PERSPECTIVES ON THE
SOCIAL SCIENCES IN CANADA

T0324430

EDITED BY
T.N. GUINSBURG AND G.L. REUBER

Perspectives on the
Social Sciences in Canada

UNIVERSITY OF TORONTO PRESS

© University of Toronto Press 1974
Toronto and Buffalo
Reprinted in paperback 2017

ISBN 978-0-8020-2164-9 (cloth)
ISBN 978-0-8020-6248-2 (paper)
LC 74-78508

Contents

Contributors

W.P. ARCHIBALD Assistant Professor of Sociology, University of Western Ontario

R. COOK Professor of History and Social Science, York University

P. DANSEREAU Professor of Ecology, Université du Québec à Montréal

J. FREEDMAN Lecturer in Anthropology, University of Western Ontario

M.F. GOODCHILD Associate Professor of Geography, University of Western Ontario

T.N. GUINSBURG Associate Professor of History and Assistant Dean of Social Science, University of Western Ontario

H.G. JOHNSON Professor of Economics, London School of Economics and University of Chicago

N. KEYFITZ Andelot Professor of Demography and Sociology, Harvard University; formerly Senior Research Statistician, Dominion Bureau of Statistics, Ottawa

C.B. MACPHERSON Professor of Political Science, University of Toronto

G.L. REUBER Professor of Economics and Dean of Social Science, University of Western Ontario

M. ROKEACH Professor of Sociology and Psychology, Washington State University

Y.F. ZOLTVANY Associate Professor of History, University of Western Ontario

Preface

The papers included in this volume were originally presented, in somewhat different form, at a conference to commemorate the opening of the Social Science Centre at the University of Western Ontario in the spring of 1973. Participants were asked to take stock of the development of their disciplines in Canada, to assay the contours of current endeavours, and to comment upon avenues of future research. As the papers demonstrate, not all of the invited scholars chose to interpret the mandate in quite the same way. This diversity itself probably says something about the nature of the social sciences, and we believe that it added to the interest of the conference and of the present volume. We have also included most of the commentaries on the papers that were made by the conference speakers and the invited discussants from Western's social-science faculty. Unfortunately we were unable to include the stimulating question-and-answer sessions that followed the papers or the informal colloquies touched off by them, both of which confirmed our notion that the papers should reach a wider audience.

We wish to express appreciation to Mr Donald J. Smith of London, Ontario, for financing the conference at which these papers were first presented and for funds to help support their publication.

TNG GLR

University of Western Ontario
London, Canada
August 1973

PERSPECTIVES ON THE
SOCIAL SCIENCES IN CANADA

T.N. GUINSBURG
G.L. REUBER

Introduction

The social sciences constitute an extended family, whose members, even if they reside under one roof, live in a relationship with one another that is sometimes competitive, other times disdainful, and too seldom mutually supportive. While all the disciplines have professed a common goal – the 'proper study of mankind' – each has sought to carve out a special niche for itself, often at the expense of others, producing in the process a particularized approach to the study of society, a special methodology, and often, alas, a distinctive if not distinguished language. Consequently, much as the desirability of communicating with one another has become manifest, the difficulty of doing so successfully has increased. To compound the problem, the individual disciplines in the social sciences have themselves fragmented, to the point where even those referred to by the same disciplinary name often seem to have very little in common. Symposia on the social sciences can serve to illuminate these problems and perhaps, ultimately, to help mitigate them.

This collection of papers, however, is not a symposium on the overall condition of the social sciences. Rather it is an assessment of some of the social sciences in Canada, an inquiry somewhat less audacious but nonetheless complex. Although making many penetrating observations on the social science disciplines *per se*, the contributors render their greatest service by analysing the nature of social-science scholarship within and about Canada. In various ways the authors address themselves to one or more of the following matters: the degree to which the disciplines as practised in Canada are linked to or differentiated from their practice elsewhere; the benefits and drawbacks of a 'nationalistic' approach to scholarship in the social sciences; the contributions of Canadian scholarship to the study of society in general and Canadian society in particular; the interaction among the social sciences in Canada and the need for interdisciplinary studies; and the unfulfilled agenda of Canadian social science.

To their credit, the authors of these essays do not produce panegyrics to their disciplines or to the Canadian practice thereof. Not that they are doleful about the present or the future; indeed, most are optimistic. But even as they appreciate the forward strides taken in their disciplines in recent years, these scholars decry the shortcomings and warn of the pitfalls. They recognize that, as in many areas of modern civilization, quantitative growth has outstripped qualitative performance.

Quantitatively, no one would deny that the social sciences in Canada have leapt forward. In each of the disciplines assessed, recent growth has been striking if not astounding. Professor Macpherson's statement that in the two main fields of political science more doctoral theses were in progress in 1971-2 than were completed in the previous half-century is but the most arresting of the indices of growth that could be mustered for each of the subject areas. University and governmental employment of social scientists has burgeoned, scholars have moved into new fields of specialization, and their researches have poured forth faster than presses could accommodate them.

The strengths and weaknesses of this unprecedented expansion preoccupy each of the contributors to this volume. Although the authors do not use identical criteria for evaluating scholarly merit, and are not equally severe in such evaluations, all the essays point out the ways in which the practice of Canadian scholarship might more closely approach its potential. If Professors Keyfitz and Cook, for example, are less radical in their critical strictures than Macpherson is, the former still register pointed and constructive suggestions for enhancing the agenda of their disciplines.

In probing the nature and explanation of the perceived deficiencies, most of the papers find it appropriate to discuss the relationship of the discipline in Canada to the discipline at large. Is there a distinctive Canadian character in the social sciences? The scholars represented here seem to agree that there is not, but they by no means concur on whether such lack of national distinctiveness is lamentable. For Professor Johnson, economics in Canada is not really separable from the overall development of economic science, and it would be regrettable if it were. Professor Macpherson, on the other hand, grieves that the 'possessive individualist' culture of contemporary North American society has succeeded in contaminating Canadian political science. Others take a middle position, contending that while the social sciences in Canada have benefited appreciably – particularly in methodology – from their international connections, there is a vast potential, largely untapped thus far, for distinctive Canadian investigations of a variety of problems for which Canadian society furnishes a 'natural laboratory'.

In any event, as one reflects upon the papers presented here, it becomes apparent that Canada has rarely developed identifiable 'schools of thought' – such has have arisen at various times and places in Europe and the United States – in any of the social sciences. Canadian social science has characteristically been eclectic rather than dogmatic and revolutionary. In part this may reflect its pragmatic rather than philosophical outlook. And it may provide an important clue in explaining why few, if any, Canadian social scientists are seen, either at home or abroad, as pioneers in the theoretical development of their subjects. While this feature might be regrettable in some respects, it might also have some redeeming features. One may be that teaching and research in the social sciences tend to be somewhat less narrowly cast in Canada than abroad. Canadian social scientists, moreover, perhaps direct a larger share of their activities to the study of Canadian society than they would if their bent were more philosophical.

If the testimony of the participants in this symposium is correct, the social sciences in Canada have the capacity to contribute to an international body of learning as well as to a deeper understanding of past and present Canadian society. In pursuit of these dual goals, the papers suggest, social scientists in Canada must be conscious of the milieu in which they work, yet must also be eclectic. They must hold in balance the desire to create a distinctive Canadian social science and the desire to avoid parochialism. While most of the papers express the hope that scholarship emanating from Canada will make an increasingly large impact, none of the authors – all but one native Canadians – shows great concern that Canada, because of the relative youth and the previously small scale of its graduate programs, has thus far imported considerable academic talent. Many of these scholars, it is noted, have greatly enhanced the development of the social sciences in Canada, and as Professor Rokeach seeks to demonstrate, academic values transcend national boundaries. Even in understanding the Canadian scene, Professor Keyfitz suggests, 'outsiders' frequently can offer acute observations, and there is no reason that outsiders cannot join with insiders in advancing the frontiers of Canadian scholarship.

Collectively, this group of essays paints an exciting landscape of the social sciences in Canada during the years ahead. Even the mere mention of a few prominent features of this landscape is exhilarating: the social psychology of biculturalism, the study of nationalism as a social phenomenon, analysis of the socio-economic foundations of the political structure, investigations of migrant assimilation, and historical studies of the social, professional, economic and intellectual roots of Canadian society, to name just a few. But the listing of such projects leads to still another query: Can any of these endeavours be successfully undertaken if the social sciences proceed in their accelerating compartmentalization and internal fragmentation?

Scholarship in any segment of the social-science family necessarily is based on many assumptions drawn from others. Because of imperfect knowledge and compartimentalization, the assumptions made in one sector all too often reflect outdated or erroneous views of the state of knowledge in others. The papers presented here reflect this difficulty at a number of points. As the social sciences in Canada strive for greater cohesion and interaction, it will become increasingly important and difficult for scholars in one area to keep abreast of the rapidly growing contemporary scholarship developed in other areas – an undertaking quite distinct from interdisciplinary studies.

Throughout this volume runs a leitmotif – that toilers in the social science vineyards isolate themselves only at great peril. Though such warnings are not new, amid the recent 'professionalization' of most of the social sciences they have largely gone unheeded. Consequently, whatever unity once existed in the study of man and his institutions has

vanished. The various social scientists, however professionally competent, have found it increasingly difficult to see life steadily and see it
whole. Thus Macpherson yearns for the days when, he believes, the
study of political economy made possible more realistic analysis than do
the divorced disciplines of political science and economics. Similarly,
Rokeach finds it appalling that social psychologists in sociology and
those in psychology go about their work in mutual exclusiveness. The
others, too, warn of the danger that intellectual myopia in their fields
may result in more and more knowledge of less and less significance.

None of the scholars would deny the virtues, pointed out by Adam
Smith long ago, of division of labour; nor would they discount the
increments to knowledge resulting from increasing specialization and
sophistication within the social sciences. They insist, however, that this
knowledge will be of minuscule value if it is not related to large questions and theories of human behaviour, a quest that can only be frus-
trated and obstructed by intradisciplinary and interdisciplinary fragmentation. Consequently, though all of these scholars, for obvious
reasons, exhibit strong pride in their disciplines, they generally concede
that their craft, at its best, must be broad-gauged. While Professor
Cook, for example, cautions his fellow historians about concluding that
borrowing techniques and concepts from other disciplines automatically produces better history, he asserts that historians of Canada
can best pursue the sociocultural questions heretofore neglected by
absorbing such techniques and insights. It is increasingly apparent that
the scholar must be willing not only to leave the cozy confines of his
own office and department but even to venture outside the social-
science building.

Just how 'scientific' the social sciences can and should be is, of
course, itself a matter of some controversy. All of the social scientists
here represented recognize the advances made in their disciplines by the
introduction of sophisticated quantitative and empirical techniques.
Yet each of them, to a greater or lesser degree, betrays discernible
wariness of the exaltation of technique at the expense of imagination.
Professor Keyfitz, himself one of the most gifted of mathematically
oriented sociologists, clearly recognizes that the most refined of
methodologies will yield very little unless the right questions are posed.
As Ramsay Cook avows that historians will never exchange their

humanistic heritage for a 'mess of value-free social-science pottage,' so Brough Macpherson assails most of his colleagues in political science for having done just that. If the computer has come to symbolize the 'new' social science, these scholars know that despite its machinations, there will always be limits to exactitude in the study of man and society. Many questions – some would say most of the truly important ones – are not susceptible to scientific verification. But such inherent limits, the papers suggest, will not prevent the ablest social scientists from seeking to use the most rigorous methodologies available.

Yet another problem for the social sciences, though not fully dealt with in these papers, is the sensitive and difficult relationship between social science and the social scientists, on the one hand, and society and its government, on the other. This complicated issue is considered at length in only one of the papers – significantly perhaps, the paper on economics, which at present is probably the most directly applicable of the social sciences to policy issues, and the practitioners of which have had the closest contact with government. It has long been recognized, of course, that the social sciences face an inherent difficulty: the investigator is frequently part of the society that he is studying and consequently is likely to find it more difficult to attain the same degree of critical detachment from the objects of his investigation than, say, a chemist investigating molecular structure. This general difficulty for the social sciences is enormously compounded in the present situation where virtually all teaching and research are funded in one way or another by the government, where the largest employer of qualified social scientists outside the universities is the government, and where the greatest scope for the application of knowledge developed in the social sciences is within governmental circles. The attempts that have been made to establish endowed institutions more truly independent of government and business influence have foundered, evidently because neither governments (and their officials) nor businessmen, on whom the provision of adequate endowments largely depends, have been prepared to see such an institution let loose in the country without strings attached.

While this situation undoubtedly has complex explanations – touched upon by Professor Macpherson – among which are direct pressures from vested interests, it may partly reflect scepticism on the part of many persons, including many intellectuals, about the motivations, methods and findings of social-science research and the value of training in this area. Society's problems — economic, political, and social — seem to mock the alleged expertise and high flown theories of those who call themselves social scientists. Though this fact alone may not justify disparaging the value of the social sciences, the widespread scepticism in the community makes it very important that social scientists in Canada and elsewhere strive both to raise their standards of scholarship and to convince society that their work is not divorced from reality. Although this in itself will not resolve the difficult relationship between social scientists and governments, it will at least reduce the cogency of one of the arguments most frequently invoked against social scientists.

The agenda spelled out here for the social sciences in Canada will not be easy to follow. The problems are many — and are not confined to Canadian quarters. But the papers presented here suggest that the Canadian branch of the social-science family, if it is to achieve the goals within its grasp, must above all take steps to abolish senseless internecine conflict and smug self-satisfaction among its members. It can neither isolate itself intellectually nor permit its members to lose sight of their common concerns. Not that scholarly identities will or can be subsumed; the papers and commentaries herein make that clear. But, as Professor Rokeach suggests in the concluding sentence of his essay, unless social scientists in Canada and elsewhere come to recognize that their individual achievements can only be weakened by academic egocentrism and ethnocentrism, centres for social sciences cannot be transformed from houses to homes.

N. KEYFITZ

1
Sociology and Canadian society

Sociology in recent years has been called on to answer many practical questions, some of them concerning deep-seated difficulties of advanced industrial society, probably unanswerable in the present state of knowledge. Serious workers in the discipline give no encouragement to those who look to it for fast solutions to unsolvable problems. A popularity based on unrealistic expectations will prove fragile, and sociologists respond by using relatively precise methods to attack smaller questions that they hope are not intractable.

They are encouraged by the degree to which a sociological approach has spread through many fields. History, anthropology, political science, and other disciplines have learned from sociology how to look at their materials. The penetration of sociology into diverse subject matter has produced everything from a sociology of science, through a sociology of economic life, to a sociology of revolution. The official sociology of current journal articles has reached a new high level of sophistication in dealing with empirical data. Based on the practical and theoretical questions asked of it, and the research techniques it has contributed, sociology is successful as never before on several criteria of success – number of faculty and students, volume of publication, size and wealth of clientele.

But the successes are balanced by weaknesses, especially the fragmentation into a host of subdisciplines which are only partially intercommunicating. Not only are substantive interests widely dispersed, but viewpoints differ considerably on any one subject, and even a common language in which differences could be effectively discussed is hard to find.

The sociologies of the main centres – the United States, England, France, Germany, and Canada – have much in common, but they are distinguished from one another as well. In each of these five countries sociology is related to the other social sciences in somewhat different ways, and each takes some of its problems from national concerns. But Canadian subjects of investigation have been similar to those of the United States. This is an opportunity lost in so far as Canadian society has distinctive features and problems which should instigate new and important work. The point applies less to French than to English work; the sociology departments of Laval and the University of Montreal seem to be developing in parallel to the development of French-Canadian society.

This paper will attempt to characterize sociology as practised in North America and Europe, and then sketch five topics in incipient Canadian sociology, and will end with some remarks on the degree to which sociology can be nation-free.

NORTH AMERICA

Among many other matters, North American sociology is concerned with race, cities and poverty (Greer 1965; Martin 1961), crime (Bell 1960; Skolnick 1966; Westley 1953), and population. Yet these matters, as observed and analysed in the United States, are exotic in relation to Canada. Canada has no problem of Blacks and Whites. Neighbourhoods in Canadian cities are more stable; it is much easier in Montreal than in Chicago to point to areas in which the physical structures, and the social class that inhabits them, have been substantially unchanged for half a century. If that process of metabolism by which neighbourhoods deteriorate, are levelled to the ground, are rebuilt, and deteriorate again occurs in Canadian cities, it does so in a much slower rhythm.

Another aspect of American life that Canada does not fully share is crime. Canadian crime rates are much lower: for example, in 1969 Canada had 341 murders compared with 14,480 in the United States, according to the official yearbooks. Lynn McDonald (1969, p.212) tells us that the crime rate in Canada has remained constant during the 1960s; this is a further mark of difference between the two countries of North America. Canada may still be sufficiently backward, its people still sufficiently law-abiding, that the traditional threat system of the law continues to be operative, and the theory can be maintained that every violator of every existing law is prosecuted. With a credible threat system, enforcement is cheap enough that limitation of resources does not impose decisions about which laws to retain and which to abandon.

On any list of themes of North American sociology we have no difficulty in citing references to Canadian scholars as well as to those from the United States: the sociology of work (Hughes 1958; Westley and Westley 1971); of medicine (Hall 1948; Brazeau 1961); of other professions and professions in general (McFarlane 1965; Parsons 1964, p.34); of the labour force (Hauser 1964; Hamilton 1973); of politics (Lipset 1960; Meisel 1967); of the military (Janowitz 1960; Solomon 1961; Jones 1961); of everyday life (Lefebvre 1958; Goffman 1971; Zakuta 1970); of the community (Lynd 1929; Seeley et al. 1956); of the family (Goode 1964; Garigue 1962; Carisse 1970); of internal and external migration (Stone 1969; Petersen 1955; Kalbach 1969); of advertising (Elkin 1973); of social mobility (Sorokin 1964; Porter 1968; Breton 1972), and many others.

It is enough to say here that in every one of scores of such specialties a new perspective is provided by considering individual activities in relation to group life. Where common sense sees the doctor's actions as determined wholly by the technical requirements of healing, and leisure activities as sheer individual spontaneity, the sociologist is perpetually able to surprise by showing how group norms, institutions, and interests intervene. For him things are not what they seem. Neither are things what they seem to other scientists, political analysts, or literary critics, but the surprises of the sociologist extend over an especially wide range of substantive interests, and they are objectively confirmed by relatively hard data. This is the success story of sociology, of which the obverse is fragmentation.

A part of the success rests on the empiricism of contemporary sociology. If subject matter is a centrifugal influence, do not methods, at least, give us something in common?

EMPIRICAL STUDY AND MATHEMATICAL THEORY

Though students and the public turn to sociology for answers to pressing questions on crime, poverty, and population, sociologists are
modest about their present ability to give answers. Certainly the main
content of the official journals is not articles on how to deal with
poverty or how to deal with crime. What sociologists think they have
done best, and what fills the journals, is the analysis of empirical data.
The technique for this and the substantive results based on it constitute
the most characteristic achievement of sociology.

The start of empirical study in sociology is the framing of propositions that risk being rejected by observation. Homans's famous 'If the
frequency of interaction between two or more persons increases, the
degree of their liking for one another will increase' (1950, p.112) requires for its testing only that 'frequency of interaction' and 'liking' be
measured over some population. The proposition can be joined with
others, as was done by Herbert Simon (1957) in a mathematical formulation. The theory constituted by Simon's differential equations
permits a chain of inferences which does not become weak because it is
long. The equations are a language which transcends the boundaries of
disciplines and of nations. Errors expressed in equations stand out more
sharply than errors expressed in words.

Harrison C. White (1962) shows how kinship lines and relationships
can be traced without difficulty by matrix manipulation, and his results
make kinship more understandable to anthropologists. White (1970)
also studied chains of opportunity: the sequence of events when worker
A leaves his job and is replaced by B, B's job is filled by C, C's job by D,
etc. Such a chain applies to housing accommodation, taxi utilization,
and other phenomena.

Goodman (1965) and others have studied mobility; competing
models include a heterogeneous population consisting of two groups
called movers and stayers respectively, and a homogeneous population
in which the chance that a person will stay where he is increases with
the length of time he has been there. Coleman (1964), in what remains
the standard book on mathematical sociology, shows how migration
can be expressed as a stochastic process, how sociometric graphs (who
is friends with whom) can be represented by matrices whose powers

give friends of friends, etc. Keyfitz (1968) has assembled in one place the mathematics by which population dynamics is analysed. Mathematical sociology is now important enough to have a journal devoted to it.

Jean-Paul Sartre (1960, p.50), hardly biased in favour of American culture or institutions, speaks in unexpectedly laudatory terms of American sociology: 'Aux USA, la sociologie se développe en raison de son efficacité même ... Si c'est une arme efficace – et elle a prouvé qu'elle en était une – c'est qu'elle est vraie en quelque mesure; et si elle est "aux mains des capitalistes", c'est une raison de plus pour la leur arracher at la retourner contre eux.'

The social sciences all try to make statistical data speak to questions of causation. Notwithstanding Hume's proof that causal inference is impossible, everyone engages in it, scientists more than most other people. Random allocation of treatments to subjects is one solution: if we could take a number of children and randomly determine which of them would go to college and which go to work at age seventeen, and then compare incomes twenty years later, we would know how much income to impute to college education. Since this method is wholly impracticable, we have to use passive observation, and the result is always subject to interference by associated variables. If those who go to college come from wealthy homes, then we face the question of whether their subsequent higher incomes are due to their college attandance or to their parents' incomes. But this problem could be overcome by holding parents' incomes constant, in other words comparing college and non-college persons among a group whose parents' incomes are the same. And we could similarly find the effect of parents' income with college attendance held constant, and so separate the effects of the two factors. Multiple regression is a way of achieving the same allocation of causal influence with greater economy of data (though with some extra assumptions), and like multiple classification it permits holding constant any extraneous variable that can be named and measured.

The method of path coefficients (Duncan 1966) deals with the further complication that the explaining variables act on one another as well as on the one that is to be explained. Duncan shows that if a causal ordering of the variables may be assumed (and this is often unambiguous – my father's schooling could have affected mine, but mine could not possibly have affected my father's) then the extent of influence of each one of a very complex pattern of variables on the others can be estimated statistically by a suitable arrangement of regression equations. Goodman (1972) has developed the theory in general form, and though no one can break through the ultimate logical ceiling on causal knowledge set by Hume, his and Duncan's work is pressing hard against that ceiling. A critical review of methods for the inference of causality is provided by Serge Carlos (1970, p.189).

The important point is that causality is specifiable only within a model, and different models of the same reality provide different causal relations. As a recent example (Easterlin 1973), we find that at any one time persons of higher income report fewer worries and preoccupations, a condition that, for brevity, can be called happiness. On this evidence alone, the way to increase the happiness of the population is to increase its average income. But suppose that the happiness of those with more income is due only to their relative position – to their seeing less well-off people around them. Then raising all incomes in proportion would have no effect on happiness. Easterlin's analysis of time-series and inter-country comparisons shows little variation in the distribution of happiness from time to time, though the correlation with income at any one time is very persistent. The measurement of happiness is not easy; suffice it here that the data selected and the way it is thought about affect decisively the causal conclusion drawn; increasing aggregate income increases happiness on one model, leaves happiness unchanged on another.

Mathematical language and the application of empirical data are associated with one another in sociology as they are in physics. A chain of reasoning in which each proposition is necessary and sufficient for the others not only provides causal explanation, but offers the advantage that verification at any point in the chain verifies the whole. Verification has occurred when a proposition has been confronted with data that could have proved it wrong but did not. And since the confrontation is difficult to arrange one must derive the maximum benefit from any successful accomplishment of it. That is what theory does, and mathematical theory does it best. The perennial trouble is coaxing problems into mathematical form. The scholar too often has to choose between providing precise answers to uninteresting questions and vague answers to important ones.

Anyone who has followed the main journals since World War II notes the very considerable change in the presentation of research consequent on application of these techniques. Some were already known in genetics, econometrics and psychology, but they had to be adapted for use in sociology. Their diffusion into our discipline has been helped by the grants economy that greatly increased the ability of scholars to gather directly the primary data suited to their own problems. The surveys of childbearing conducted by Norman Ryder and his colleagues (Ryder and Westoff 1971) are a major example of large-scale data-gathering operations to provide knowledge of the interrelations of social variables. The official journals show the degree to which grants have pushed in the direction of empiricism.

That trend is not to the taste of all sociologists. Some charge that data-gathering can be actively harmful: for example, study of the poor helps the authorities to manipulate them in situations of class conflict; corporation boards, the federal cabinet, and other elite groups are not as open with data that would enable the poor to manipulate *them*. (The thought is implicit in the words of Sartre quoted earlier.) Some say more broadly that empirical work is bound to be conservative; positive value-free study of what *is* does not reveal the defects of reality; we should study what is in the light of what *ought to be*. Others complain that empirical work is concerned with trivial details, that it is intended to satisfy the terms of grants and contracts and that the manner of administration of these is such that they can be satisfied without adding very much to knowledge.

UNIFICATION

Despite these objections raised by many students and some faculty, a common skill in methods is urged as a means of making sociology a profession as well as a discipline. If all those with a Ph D could be certified as having such a skill, they could be looked to for the execution of surveys, the presentation of the results of surveys, the devising and fitting of models to data arising from surveys, the inference of causal relations from such data. Some numbers appear in 90 per cent of the articles in the official journals, and 60 per cent of a sample I counted use advanced statistical techniques.

From this point of view ideal training is provided as a part of graduate work at the National Opinion Research Center of the University of Chicago, the Bureau of Applied Social Research at Columbia, the Survey Research Center of the University of Michigan, and in Canada at the Survey Research Centre of York University and the Centre de Sondage of the University of Montreal. Associated with survey work is skill in computer operation and programming. Nonnumerical application of computers is a natural extension; it has been useful in sociometric work and has greatly increased the potency of content analysis in the hands of Philip Stone (1966) and others. With such skills sociology could become a profession having a large fraction of its members in business and government. But sociology as a whole does not seem to be taking this direction (Janowitz 1972).

The fragmentation of sociology consequent on its success in many diverse fields may be overcome by an overriding theory, in so far as it cannot be overcome by methodology and professionalization. The dominating theory has been that of Talcott Parsons, who over the three decades that started with *The Structure of Social Action* (1936) has evolved a highly original synthesis of the classics of sociology. Parsons has in common with the very different sociologies of Homans (1950) and Blau (1964) an emphasis on exchange, but in his case it takes place especially between the analytically separate functional subsystems. His is a theory for a plural society in which social order is problematic. A recent intellectual autobiography (Parsons 1970) throws light on the sources of Parsonian theory. An important evaluation has recently appeared in France, written by a Canadian authority (Rocher 1972).

The notion that Parsons's way of doing sociology is conservative has persisted from Mills (1959) through Wrong (1961) to Gouldner (1970). Lipset and Ladd (1972) show how contrary to fact is the charge of conservatism. Only to be tested by future application of Parsons's framework is Homans's view (1964) that one can get down to the work of concrete social analysis as well without it.

An alternative means of unification in the history of ideas tradition has come from Robert Nisbet (1966). But we must leave this difficult subject and go on to look at the different national forms into which contemporary sociology is pressed.

AN INTERNATIONAL COMPARISON

If American sociology is diverse, methodology-oriented, productive, and confident, British sociology is diffident, pensive, and eclectic, French deals boldly with large units, German continues to be historical. These points require some elaboration before we examine the national character of Canadian sociology.

The *British Journal of Sociology* is less empirical and methodological than the corresponding *American Sociological Review*. It discusses different questions – concerning, for instance, the origins of sociology and its relation to epistemology. For good or for ill, sociology in the United States is sufficiently entrenched that it is no longer concerned to establish its own position. These and similar topics fit into the British humane academic tradition and give, to American eyes, a philosophical tinge to the *Journal*.

Even more insistence that there be no sharp boundary between sociology on the one hand and philosophy, history, and other disciplines on the other is found in Germany. In a controversy over method between Theodore W. Adorno (1972) and Karl Popper, the latter (representing positivism) agreed with his opponent that any line between sociology and philosophy would become a trench into which both would fall. Interest in the supra-empirical question whether we are now in the epoch of late (and declining) capitalism or of early (and rising) post-industrial society has been formally debated by Adorno and Ralf Dahrendorf. For the former, classes (with collective interests that transcend the material gain of their members) remain the essence of the contemporary social structure; for the latter, classes dissolve and disappear under modern methods of production and rising incomes. Sociologists at Frankfurt, like Ludwig von Friedebourg, have been interested in industrial sociology, and their writing has something in common with American work on human relations in industry, but lacks most of the attention to subjective features of conduct. Jürgen Ritsert (1972) applies content analysis and associates it with ideology.

Starting in history, German social science doubts whether there can be social laws invariant over all historical epochs. The issue has found one resolution on this side of the Atlantic in confining research to theories of the middle range. Here as on other points, German sociology, in the critical school of Adorno centred in Frankfurt (Adorno 1972) deals at least partly with issues similar to those of standard American sociology, and the discussion goes on in a parallel terminology. Thus the contradictions, the unravelling of which is the task of critical sociology, are dysfunctions in our language; the reflexive character of critical sociology, its taking account of the social consequences of its own findings, is for us exemplified by the self-fulfilling prophecy; that institutions serve hidden purposes, and that individuals and groups are deceived by ideologies that bring about false consciousness of their own interests, appears in the contrast between manifest and latent functions (Merton 1957). Marx's *praxis* (Habermas 1972) is one of a number of pragmatisms; Dewey's is another; they are applied in contemporary American action-research.

Thus German sociology, even of the Frankfurt school, which calls itself critical (that is, stemming from Marx), is not as sharply differentiated from American sociology as the respective vocabularies might suggest. The more empirical Cologne school is even less differentiated. Yet a glance at any current journal shows some differences both in methods of research and in the selection of problems.

Frenchmen have sought logic and generality, in contrast to the German tendency to embed social science in history. Thus French structuralism, in a line of parentage that runs back through Levi-Strauss, Durkheim, and Comte, looks for extra-historical social configurations and studies relations among them. But the Marxist revival, necessarily historical, is common to France and Germany. The attempt to reconcile Marxism with the somewhat opposite structuralism – an attempt that includes the work of Althusser and many others – has animated much of French sociology since World War II.

CANADIAN SOCIOLOGY

Canada has three journals of sociology. The *Canadian Review of Sociology and Anthropology* is the official organ of the national association and carries articles in French as well as English. *Recherches sociographiques*, founded at Laval in the late 1950s, concentrates on Quebec society; in the theory-description continuum it stays near the description end, at least for the present holds back on theorizing, and is building a solid base of Quebec materials. *Sociologie et sociétés*, published in Montreal, the first issues of which is dated May 1969, is closer to the theory end of the continuum, and its subject matter is less specifically Quebec-oriented; it brings the flavour of European thought to North American sociology with articles on ideology, alienation, political participation, and other topics of what one writer calls critical as opposed to aseptic sociology.

COMPARISON OF CANADIAN AND AMERICAN SOCIOLOGY

If a characteristic Canadian sociology exists it should be revealed in the official journal. I took the issues of the *Canadian Review of Sociology and Anthropology* for the years 1969 and 1970 and examined the authorship of the forty-eight articles and notes that they contained. Of the forty-eight, thirty-seven were by writers living in Canada, the rest by residents of the United States. There was a slight concentration among the institutions represented: Queen's showed five contributions; McGill, Toronto, and Alberta four each; McMaster and Memorial three each; the others showed two or less. New universities are well represented. The large extent to which sociology is academic is shown by the fact that all but one of the thirty-seven pieces were written by members of a university or other teaching institution, and the one exception was written by an officer of a teachers' association.

That the academic addresses of over three-quarters of the writers were in Canada makes it effectively a Canadian journal, and that they were widely dispersed makes it an all-Canadian journal, reflecting a fair dispersion of sociologists and anthropologists as a whole through the country. Taking the 1035 listed members of the Canadian Sociology and Anthropology Association according to its 1970 directory, Ontario leads with 457 members, and the Atlantic provinces are at the bottom with seventy. As a demographer I report these numbers in relation to population. My calculation puts Ontario at the top with sixty-one dues-paying sociologists and anthropologists per million population, and the Atlantic provinces and Quebec at the bottom with thirty-five each. (Quebec undoubtedly contains many French-speaking sociologists who are not members of the CSAA.) The prairie provinces and British

Columbia come in the middle with forty-eight and fifty-nine sociologists and anthropologists respectively per million population. The American Sociological Association shows 12,903 members for 1969, including about 600 Canadians but not including anthropologists. The United States thus has about sixty sociologists per million, a somewhat greater density than Canada's, corresponding to the American excess in university enrolment and faculty in all fields. Sociology seems to have about the same relative place in the academic life of the two countries.

For a number of members the directory gives the degree and the place where it was taken. The overwhelming proportion of this non-random sample have degrees from American universities, some from European, a few from Canadian. In the past Canada has trained few of its own faculty, but this situation is changing rapidly. Of fifty-five doctoral degrees expected to be granted to Canadians in 1971-2, fully thirty-four are from Canadian universities, only thirteen from American (Ostry 1972, p.126).

We have seen that Canadian sociology is separate from that of the United States in the sense that it has its official journal and the journal is three-quarters written by faculty in Canadian universities. We are given no indication of how many of the writers are American-born and American citizens, but we suspect that the fraction is large, especially in western Canada. For the whole of the social sciences no region outside of Quebec shows as many as two-thirds Canadian citizens among faculty in the social sciences, and the western region shows only about half (Ostry, p.124). For sociology and anthropology, the fraction is only 40.3 per cent, against 38.5 per cent United States citizens (Ostry, p.96). The number of American-born faculty teaching in Canadian universities is probably greater than the number of Canadian-born in American universities, though I have no data on this. Certainly the Canadians in the United States, being distributed among an indigenous population ten times as large, are less conspicuous. I have never heard any suggestion that Canadians are clogging the American university system and blocking the advance of native Americans. Here as elsewhere the irritations of continentalism are less pronounced in the United States.

Canada has always been a part of the system of pathways over which North American scholars, as itinerant as those of the Middle Ages, have circulated. But with some freezing of the channels in the United States, the waters have backed up into Canada, a demographic-economic hazard with considerable consequences for Canadian nationalism. Things have changed enough that not all young people would share Claude Bissell's calm and liberal view of a few years back, written at a time when Canadian universities were hiring thirty or more sociologists per year and producing fewer than half a dozen PhDs. After speaking of the brain drain to the United States he says, 'There is no need for alarm, provided that there is a compensating movement back to Canada of American academics and professionals' (Bissell 1967, p.190). Now the supply of Canadian PhDs in sociology is estimated at forty-seven, and the demand for them between thirteen and twenty-eight (Ostry 1972, p.102). A rough indication of the accelerating prospective output of Canadian teachers is given by Canada Council fellowships in sociology, tenable in Canada or abroad, which rose from thirty-nine in 1965-6 to 165 in 1970-1. Will there be posts in the United States for those unplaced in Canada?

The articles in the Canadian *Review* are on subjects that appear in American journals and do not differ greatly in quality. That most sociologists in English Canada were trained in the United States has clearly affected their choice of problems. If there is any difference it is in the greater emphasis on methodology in the major American journals. The only feature that would tell the reader that the *Review* is Canadian, if that were not indicated on the cover, is that some articles have a Canadian locale, for example, 'Social Class and Segregation within Ethnic Groups in Toronto'. Just as between the two countries problems are the same, method is the same (but perhaps less statistical in Canada), and substantive differences are in locale at most. The integration of Canadian with American sociology is especially emphasized by references and citations, the great majority in the *Review* being to American journals and books. The *Review* is also cited in American journals, but less often, so that the integration is asymmetric.

No one to whom I have spoken was willing to consider the Canadian *Review* as representing Canadian sociology. Articles are selected from some larger set by their authors and editors according to criteria not easily set down. For this reason and other complex ones, graduate and undergraduate courses are not centred on journal articles either current or past; this is true both in Canada and in the United States. Teaching is important in Canada: Desmond Connor and James Curtis (1970) show the number and range of sociology programs. Taught sociology is conveyed by course outlines, by student work in courses, by textbooks and by selections of readings. Some student essays have been made available (for instance, Jonassohn 1972), and their descriptions of racetrack gamblers, the death of a newspaper, a women's commune, have an immediacy not to be found in official journals. Canadian textbooks are not much in evidence; their place tends to be taken by selections of readings, of which a number now exist.

Teaching need not leave a trace in writing. Norman Bell has taken the initiative in organizing a graduate seminar at the University of Toronto in which a number of faculty and students have participated, dealing specifically with biculturalism; Quebec lecturers have been invited, and the seminar has been climaxed by a two-day visit to the University of Montreal by the entire Toronto group.

Research sociology is represented by a growing number of monographs that I refer to in other parts of this essay. Lists of dissertations like the one compiled by Steeves (1971) are helpful. Research of the future is indicated by awards of the Canada Council (the main source of support), as published annually. Papers presented at annual meetings of the CSAA are a further means of tracing research interests.

One could argue that the United States is so big, in both intellectual and material output, that it necessarily imposes its methods as well as its subjects on sociology everywhere. But this is not quite the case. We have seen that British, French, and German sociology have their distinctive characters. I have not done the experiment, but I believe that one could put unidentified copies of articles in the *British Journal of Sociology* and the *American Sociological Review* before a panel of readers and they would for the most part discriminate correctly which was which, at least in a higher proportion of cases than between the Canadian and American *Reviews.*

The outcome of my comparison is a question: why has Canadian sociology not gone further along lines special to itself? That its practitioners are largely trained in the United States is not an answer. In so far as the training was good, in so far as it developed the sensitivity that Hughes (1971) calls the sociological eye, the foreigners should be especially capable of perceiving the characteristic features of Canadian life. At the very lowest level of motivation, one would think that the American assistant professor in a Canadian university would seek indigenous problems, if only to distinguish himself from competitors on both sides of the line. His ambition for advancement in either country would seem to be furthered by study of distinctively Canadian issues.

A POTENTIAL CANADIAN SOCIOLOGY

In order to demonstrate that there is a potential Canadian sociology – so far largely unnoticed in the Canadian *Review*, though prominent enough in other scholarly circles and in the newspapers – capable of inspiring creative research in our field, whether by Canadian-born, American-born, British-born, or other scholars, I shall briefly sketch five problems. Each has sufficient inherent ramifications to make it the focal point of many empirical and theoretical studies, and is difficult enough that I shall be fortunate even to be able to state it clearly.

Canadian distinctiveness

The first, already hinted at above, is the nature of nationalism. A Frenchman can see nationhood as the carrying of a distinctive cultural mission, based on a language wholly different from the English or the German of his neighbours, constituting a value *per se* whose preservation is an intrinsic good beyond discussion or question. Canadian nationality does not depend on cultural values grossly different from those of her neighbours. Cultures quite similar to hers are carried by the United States, England, and France. But just by virtue of the rather minute differences between Canadian French and French and between Canadian English and English or American (Orkin 1970, 1971), Canada offers a possibility of studying nationalism as a social phenomenon in its purest form, virtually abstracted from cultural distinctiveness. Comparative studies are suggested in which nationalism is perceived as being both *for* something and *against* something else, in which Canadian nationalism vis-à-vis the United States would be compared and contrasted with French nationalism vis-à-vis Germany, Chinese nationalism vis-à-vis Japan.

But though the differences between Canada and the United States are small, they are not negligible. Lipset (1968, p.488) shows that

Canadians have more respect for the law – although there are considerably fewer police and lawyers per head of population in Canada, there is less crime; they are less adventurous financially, as evidenced in fewer instalment purchases and fewer holdings of stocks as against bonds; they are more inclined to accept elitism in their educational system and elsewhere; they hold more tentatively to ideals of equality and individual achievement. Lipset's study was carried out before 1964, and subsequent changes need to be traced. Canada's political and other peculiarities are explained in terms of its history as a colony by Don Whyte (1973) and in terms of regional variation by Mildred Schwartz (1968, p.308).

Canada and the United States are formally sovereign and equal. But this by no means ensures symmetry in their relations, and much Canadian concern goes into avoiding a marginal position with respect to New York, Washington, Detroit, and other centres of finance, government and production. As a demonstration of one of the many ways in which the North American location is a determining factor, suppose that Canada followed Donald Creighton's advice and turned from the American dream of material affluence to some other dream of its own. Suppose that it was satisfied with half of the American income per head, but took the income in the form of greater security and a more equitable distribution of goods. The practical difficulties would start with the selective outmigration of more productive individuals, who would be able to raise their personal incomes by crossing the border, and whose departure would further lower Canadian production. For those who stayed behind the mechanism mentioned earlier, by which happiness is determined by *relative* income, would become operative; Canadians would see themselves as relatively poor in perpetuity and would be correspondingly unhappy. This would apply even though a majority of Canadians share Creighton's view. If Canada were located in Europe, with European countries as reference groups for its citizens, it would have more scope for such an un-American dream.

Within the last five years an original French-Canadian culture has started on an evolution diverging from that of France. French-Canadian speech is no longer regarded in Paris as provincial, as it was a few years back, and even less as an unsuccessful attempt to speak Parisian, but rather as a speech in its own right. French-Canadian poetry, novels, films, and television serials are appreciated in France as foreign enough to be interesting. The Parent Commission report and the Collèges d'enseignement général et professionel that emerged from it are among the models presented for French educational reforms. French Canada accepts many American elements, but it transforms them into consistency with its own norms. The recent and rapid social mobility of the middle classes in French Canada has oriented them to technology, but without weakening the traditional interest in the extended family. Few want to restore the influence of the Church in government, but a revival of personal religion is occurring among the educated. Such facts characterize a French-Canadian society admired in France for its differences as well as for its resemblances. On present trends a symmetry of mutual respect is in prospect between French Canada and France as the two cultures diverge more and more.

This cultural independence is reflected in sociology. To combine American techniques and concepts with French and apply them to the life of French Canada is the aim of researchers; the inconsistencies that make the researchers uncomfortable also make them productive. Guy Rocher is observing the educational aspirations and decisions of the young in terms of their images of the future Canadian society in a longitudinal study, employing path coefficients and other modern techniques; he finds that Quebec French youth orient to a projected future sharply different from the present, while the English of Quebec orient to a more static picture of the future. Colette Carisse is pursuing her studies of the Canadian family, Robert Sevigny (1971) of youth and the religious experience, a subject that has interested Fernand Dumont. Henripin (1971, 1972) has applied modern techniques and training to population analysis, which has been a long-standing interest of French Canada in other contexts. Attempts to study and define the global society of French Canada were discussed by Dumont (1971) a decade ago, and this is still an objective of scholarly work (Dumont and Rocher 1971).

In conversation, some Ontario sociologists have expressed envy of Quebec; when there comes to be an autonomous and unified English-Canadian society, they say, some degree of autonomy will be possible for English-Canadian sociology.

Canadian biculturalism

The Canadian public's preoccupation with French-English relations would lead us to expect many papers in the *Review* devoted to one aspect or another of such relations, but there have been very few. An early piece of Canadian field work, reported in *French Canada in Transition* (1943), was undertaken by an American, Everett Hughes, and showed important aspects of the relations of French and English in the 1920s. Hughes was inspired by Quebec, and his inspiration drove him, as often happens, to develop methods and results applicable to groups other than the one that brought them into existence. But Quebec, Canada, and the world have seen many changes in the forty years since. The pious and domesticated worker in the textile industry of 1930 has given place to a wholly new French Canadian. The earlier piety is succeeded by a quest for influence and power, not to mention the quest for an income at the North American level.

If the excitement of being an actor in influential company, of engaging in enterprises that will accomplish big things and go down in history, is found in the White House in Washington and in the board rooms of English-Canadian corporations, why should it not be found in Quebec? Gino Germani (1963) has written of the need for 'participation', as against mere income or mere voting, in Latin-American popular movements today; French Canada is not retrograde in this regard. Guy Rocher (1969) is generous in his praise of the research in sociology that the Royal Commission on Bilingualism and Biculturalism fostered and paid for. But according to him, the Commission's report suffered from a fatal defect: it disregarded the problem of power. Marcel Rioux (1969) makes the point more emphatically, Michael Oliver (1972) more calmly. English Canada had in successive steps since 1763 pushed the French language back into Quebec, treated as only one of ten provinces. Whether the French are one-tenth or one-half of Canada is no small question when interpreted as whether the French are subordinate to the English or equal to them. Sociology can investigate the two very different collective representations of this political dilemma, the one perceiving formal equality, the other perceiving colonial subordination. The turn in official policy by which the two cultures were dissolved in a multicultural Canada was distressing to many French Canadians (Rocher 1972).

Once a nation had to be homogeneous in culture; ethnic differences within nations were seen as pathological and about to disappear altogether. In the brave new world then thought to be emerging, national and possibly universal homogenization would accompany industrialism and social mobility for all. Such a process is now more often considered impoverishment, and ethnic symbols are sought and treasured. François Bourricaud shows how Indian culture in Peru is being revived to provide a richer national identity. Indian and Eskimo artifacts, as well as French, become cultural resources for all of Canada. Andrew Greeley shows the emergence of a vigorous American ethnic pluralism in the last years. For Daniel Bell and others, an ethnic group is one that emphasizes 'belonging' or 'identity'; it seems to answer both the 'Who am I' and the 'How am I regarded' questions, the Hegelian I/me distinction. In the stand against technocracy and meritocracy, identity becomes very important, and if it can be established by belonging to a subnation as well as to a nation, so much the better (*Bulletin of the American Academy of Arts and Sciences* 1973; Porter 1972).

Against such a background two societies existing within a single nation are no longer a self-contradiction, and work such as that of Guindon (1967) does not assume it to be such. Christopher Beattie (1969) analyses cooperation of French and English in the public service. Aileen Ross (1961) has carried on the work of Hughes, especially in relation to ecological succession in Quebec. John Porter (1965) has many references to the division of labour between French and English in his *Vertical Mosaic.* Jean-Charles Falardeau provides us with illuminating insights (1960).

Bilingualism as it affects communication is an inexhaustible subject of research, of which Wallace Lambert (1955, 1958) has developed some important aspects from a psychological point of view. Jacques Brazeau (1968, p.277) has written on its sociology, and the Royal Commission on Bilingualism and Biculturalism (the Dunton-Laurendeau Commission) has commissioned a number of studies, not all yet published. A whole issue of *Relations industrielles* (July 1968) was devoted to language and work; Jacques Brazeau and Jacques Dofny have studied bilingual communication in Hydro-Quebec; Frank Vallee the viability of French outside the province of Quebec.

Canadian resources

Canada is special in ways other than being a neighbour of the United States and being bilingual. It has an enormous area with corresponding resources, and a relatively small population unevenly distributed. Canadian economists have brooded over the implications of this for economic development, and a Canadian economics and economic history has arisen, expounded in the works of Harold Innis (1930) and W.T. Easterbrook (1956). The large and open landscape has produced a characteristic Canadian poetry; Douglas le Pan's *coureur de bois* 'could feed his heart on the heart of a continent'. It also influenced sociology in Carl Dawson's work on the settlement of the west (1936) and the north (1934), S.D. Clark's (1948) on religion, and Jean Burnet's (1951) on rural social organization. Seymour M. Lipset (1950) has written a classic on the spreadout societies of the prairies. But such work has attracted too few others, and the broader ecological problems have remained untouched by sociologists.

That Americans should see the resources of the continent as a unit to be exploited as quickly as possible, while Canadians are ambivalent and want to husband their resources, points to deepseated differences in ultimate goals. Do Canadians have a longer time-horizon than Americans, so that they protect their cities more against deterioration and build their houses and neighbourhoods to last longer? Canadians are economically less adventurous. They buy bonds while Americans buy stocks, all in Canadian industry and resources, and at the end of a bout of inflation the bondholders are easily paid off by the stockholders who then hold the real assets. This has been studied by a political scientist, James Eayrs (1964, p.78), who speaks of the 'innate caution of the Canadian investing temperament', but to him it is non-problematical: 'Canadians can start buying back their birthright – whenever they want to pay for it.' That economic innovation is more natural to one side of the border than the other must be related to differences in economic and social structures, and this raises non-trivial problems that deserve the attention of sociologists and other scholars.

Canada and the third world

These aspects of a Canadian sociology are related to the permanent features of Canadian life: its location alongside the United States, its large area and different goals. Only less immediately suggested is the sociology of development; one would have thought that Canadian preoccupation with developing countries would have spread over and inspired research in our discipline. The preoccupation reflects a durable difference from the United States.

The United States budget shows $80 billion for military purposes against $1.8 billion for foreign aid, a ratio of forty-five to one. The corresponding Canadian figures for 1969-70 are $1797 million and $338 million, a ratio of only five to one (*Canadian Year Book* 1970-1). Budgets speak more frankly about social goals than is customary in political and diplomatic expression, and in this instance they show that Canada has less confidence in the effectiveness of violence in international relations. Much of the relatively smaller Canadian military expenditure, moreover, is for unambiguously peacekeeping activity, studied by Solomon (1968).

Canada could have quite different policies. Within its total resources it could invade a Latin American country now and then; carry on a war in south-east Asia; possess a nuclear force at least equal to that of France. It is technically and economically capable of building a deterrent powerful enough to kill all the inhabitants of the planet. A nuclear arsenal that could kill us all twenty times over would not inspire appreciably more fear, and in this grisly equality Canada could be at the top level of world power. Once having attained such strength, it would only have to give signs of occasional erratic behaviour to become especially feared; in the balance of terror he who is dependably rational must be constantly apprehensive of his irresponsible neighbour. This is no recommendation for Canada to behave other than it does; I am only trying to establish that Canadian virtue is not the result of impotence. That Canada has not pursued international power and influence along such lines, but instead has been active in peacekeeping and puts a steadily increasing budget into foreign aid, reflects a durable preference for being liked rather than feared.

The point is well understood throughout the world, and Canadians have a unique access in Asia, Latin America, and Africa. Their contribution, on population (mentioned above) and on other subjects, would be characteristically different from that of American scholars and technicians. The Canadian government having made development a central element of its foreign policy, and the country at large having willingly assumed the mission of foreign aid, one would have anticipated a corresponding concentration of sociological research.

Certainly the problems of development are difficult enough to challenge any discipline, and they include many that fall within ours: cultural aspects of modernization, the population question, the configuration of institutions that provide a balance of social power. These have been written on by Edward Shils (1961), Philip Hauser (1969), Talcott Parsons (1960, p.98), and many others. The *Kölner Zeitschrift für Soziologie und Sozialpsychologie* has an entire volume of 800 pages (König 1969) on development. To my knowledge, John H. Kunkel (1970) is the only member of a Canadian faculty whose research has centred on this subject. Rocher's (1969) textbook deals with social change in its final volume; near the climax of the entire book is a long and thoughtful section on social and economic development. Keith Spicer (1966) has provided an impartial history of Canadian aid up to the mid-1960s.

Sociology of education

The media say much about the problems of Canadian identity. Sociologists find it hard to cope with so large and vague a subject, but they could well study the process by which the child comes to internalize Canada as a separate entity or fails to do so. And when they looked into the part that schools play in this they would find, as A.B. Hodgetts (1968) did, that the civic material served up in the schools is incoherent, low in information content, and too poorly presented to attract the interest of pupils at any level. What I heard in class in Montreal in the 1920s was not inspiring, and the improvement since has been inadequate. Canadian civic training contrasts with the intensive training in civics of American schools, where the child's assimilation of the national spirit is not left to chance (Regenstreif 1972).

The one thing that Canada has not learned from the United States is how to develop symbols that can be enduringly imprinted on the young in their first years (Porter 1967). Canadians have been less original in the creation of national symbols, as they have been with respect to symbols used to advertise consumer products. And even where Canadian symbols are perfectly satisfactory – flag and historical events, for example – they have been adopted hesitantly and are presented with diffidence. Uncertainty about nationalism is a continuing feature of the Canadian character: because parents and teachers lack the confidence to imprint their young, the young when they grow up reproduce the uncertainty, a kind of neutrality about nationhood. If such a circular tendency ever existed in the United States it was broken two centuries ago.

The sociology of education is a respectable field that deserves more research. Work has been done at the Ontario Institute for Studies in Education. Articles summarizing recent research in Quebec have been selected and presented by Belanger and Rocher (1970). In my own schooldays the boredom of the English pupils during the French lesson reflected in microcosm a central problem of the larger Canadian life. Can sociology suggest how French could be a means of communication rather than a punishment?

A DISJUNCTION BETWEEN PUBLIC CONCERN AND THE ATTENTION OF SOCIOLOGISTS

I see in each of the five fields a disjunction between public concern and research in sociology. Newspapers, magazines, radio commentators worry about Canadian identity, biculturalism, resources, foreign aid, and education, and these have been studied by sociologists, but not in proportion to the public attention. The disjunction may have been less in earlier times (Hughes 1969).

Of course a discipline does not take its subjects of research from the public, but rather from its own internal development. Scholars tackle problems arising out of the research of other scholars. Some problems are too difficult for science at a particular stage of its development; it is better to work on narrower problems that can be solved than on more important problems beyond the reach of current theory and data. But the scholarly and the public evolution cannot diverge beyond a certain point, and one has the impression that in the United States race problems, crime, the deterioration of central cities are the interest equally of the public and of sociologists.

The expansion of Canadian sociology has been very recent. Only nineteen Ph Ds were produced in Canada during the whole of the 1960s, while by 1970-1 fully 225 doctoral students were enrolled in sociology in Canadian universities (Ostry 1972, p.84). The moment for establishing a research tradition, with continuity between successive generations of teachers and students, seems to have arrived. What can be said about the relation between scholarship and nationhood?

MOVING TOWARDS A CANADIAN SOCIOLOGY

Whether sociology can be nation-free is much discussed (Naegele 1961, p.53). For Max Weber's Europe the question was whether each class should have its own sociology; for us whether each country. A sociology that will mobilize national interests is as handicapped in its search for truth as one that will mobilize class interests. But the positivistic renunciation brings dilemmas: we want knowledge in order to do something with it – to pursue some value – and even if sociologists could be disciplined to seek knowledge without ulterior purpose, such restraint cannot be expected from those who support them. Whether there can properly be a Canadian sociology is a thorny question, not to be answered with a simple yes or no. Let us tackle it under the headings of (a) methodology, (b) choice of problem, (c) choice of model, (d) accessibility to data.

If anything is international it is method. A regression is calculated the same way on both sides of the Canada-United States border; it is as place-invariant as the acceleration of a physical particle. Methods in sociometric choices, census counts, sampling theory and its application, interviewing procedures, either differ not at all or differ infinitesimally according to the country in which they are carried out. Participant observation, or Weber's ideal type (the construction of an historical individual out of the documents that history has left behind) are somewhat less determined and more often coloured by the researcher. But still most methods are relatively fixed.

Treatment of a given problem by an objective and appropriate method makes objective sociology, but the choice of problem can never be objective. A judgment on what matters are worth investigating is the first and one of the most essential of the scholar's tasks. To suppose that scholars investigate everything, that every minute study is a building block that will find a place in the structure of science at some later time so that its having no place now is no handicap, is a view that disregards the complexity of the world, the brevity of human life, the finiteness of resources for research, and the fact that social change shifts the spotlight of interest. A building block that is both practically useless now and fits into no theory or structure of knowledge now may indeed find practical or theoretical use later; history could move the spotlight of interest towards it. But it is more likely that the spotlight will move some other way. No one wants his work to be neglected, and no one makes a wholly value-free choice of his problem of investigation. National concern focuses around a set of common problems; in Canada not so much slums, race, and crime, as national unity, biculturalism, resources.

Given the problem and the internationally available stock of methods, we still have a choice of models. If we study any institution in Canada, for example trade unions or an automobile plant, our conclusions will come out one way if we treat it as autonomous, as though any links with the United States can be disregarded, and another way if we treat it as part of a larger continental entity. Study of Negroes in Nova Scotia as though they were American Blacks produces grotesque results.

John Porter and his associates point out that this kind of choice applies to my present study of sociology; on one model Canadians are contributing to a continental body of knowledge; they move easily between Canadian and American institutions of learning as students and then as teachers; journals of both countries are means of communication in an international scholarly community. On another model Canadian sociologists bear in mind that they are supported by Canada, they have a special duty to investigate the Canadian reality, and to report on it to one another and to Canadians generally. The Canadian Sociology and Anthropology Association has seen its members in both lights.

The fourth and most subtle part of the question whether sociology is nation-free is who can pursue it. If only women can understand women, only young people can understand young people, we start down a long regress, as Merton (1972) has shown. For then only young women can study young women, and further breakdown of the categories leads us to a methodological solipsism going into finer and finer groups, expressed in the phrase, 'You have to be one in order to understand one'. The sequence can only end with individual solipsism: you can only understand yourself. But we all know of instances short of psycho-analysis where others have understood us better than we understand ourselves.

For the national reality, some of the most acute observations has been by outsiders. The penetrating analysts of the United States have been de Toqueville, Lord Bryce, and Gunnar Myrdal. For Canada the corresponding service has been performed by Everett Hughes, André Siegfried and S.M. Lipset. The writings of these outsiders were accepted as the basis of the further work of insiders.

But, as Merton says, they will not always be acceptable. Ethno-centrism is not an historical constant. Under particular social conditions the insider develops the epistemological claims to privileged access to social truth. With varying degrees of intent, groups in conflict want to make their interpretation the prevailing one of how things were and are and will be. It is a short step from this to using sociology to manu-facture an ideology for the embattled group, and a short further step to making departments of sociology advanced liberated areas from which loyal followers can go forth to take over the rest of the national terri-tory. That this is the far end of a road that departs from strict posi-tivism suggests caution in travelling away from objective study. I say this not so much with the object of preserving civil order as of attaining knowledge.

ACKNOWLEDGMENT

A number of scholars have worked on updating my knowledge of socio-logy in Canada and elsewhere. I am indebted to all of them, especially Monica Boyd, Gerhard Brandt, Colette Carisse, Jacques Dofny, Frederick Elkin, Muni Frumhartz, Rudolf Gunzert, Everett C. Hughes, Kurt Jonassohn, Klaus Körber, Jacqueline Massé, Bruce McFarlane, Michael Oliver, Ian Pool, John Porter, Jürgen Ritsert, Guy Rocher, Robert Sévigny, David Solomon, William Westley, Donald Whyte, and Nur Yalman. None of them is responsible for my misunderstanding what he said.

REFERENCES

Adorno, Theodor W. 1972. *Gesammelte Schriften 8: Soziologische Schriften 1.* Frankfurt, Suhrkamp
– *et al.* 1972. *Der Positivismusstreit in der deutschen Soziologie.* Berlin, Luchterhand
Beattie, Christopher. 1969. 'Bureaucratic Careers: Middle-Level Anglophones and Francophones at Mid-career in Five Departments of the Canadian Federal Administration.' Unpublished Ph D dissertation, Department of Sociology, University of California, Berkeley
Belanger, Pierre W. and Guy Rocher, eds, 1970. *Ecole et société au Québec.* Montreal, Editions HMH
Bell, Daniel. 1960. *The End of Ideology.* New York, Collier Books
Bissell, Claude T. 1967. 'Canadian Education Today,' *Contemporary Canada*, Richard H. Leach, ed. Durham, NC, Duke University Press. Pp.177-90
Blau, Peter M. 1964. *Exchange and Power in Social Life.* New York, John Wiley & Sons
Brazeau, Jacques. 1961. 'The Practice of Medicine in Montreal,' *Canadian Society: Sociological Perspectives*, B.R. Blishen *et al.*, eds. Toronto, Macmillan Co. Pp.233-48
– 1968. 'Language Differences and Occupational Experience,' *Canada: A Sociological Profile*, W.E. Mann, ed. Toronto, Copp Clark. Pp.277-83
Breton, Raymond. 1972. *Social and Academic Factors in the Career Decisions of Canadian Youth.* Ottawa, Information Canada
Bulletin of the American Academy of Arts and Sciences. 1973. 26, p.5
Burnet, Jean. 1951. *Next-Year Country: A Study of Rural Social Organization in Alberta.* Toronto, University of Toronto Press
Canada Year Book 1970-71. Ottawa, Dominion Bureau of Statistics
Carisse, Colette. 1970. 'Family Values of Innovative Women: Perspective for the Future.' Paper prepared for delivery at the 7th World Congress of Sociology, Varna, Bulgaria
Carlos, Serge. 1970. 'Les cheminements de la causalité,' *Sociologie et sociétés, 2,* 189-201
Clark, S.D. 1948. *Church and Sect in Canada.* Toronto, University of Toronto Press
Coleman, James S. 1964. *Introduction to Mathematical Sociology.* New York, Free Press of Glencoe, Macmillan
Connor, Desmond M. and James E. Curtis. 1970. *Sociology and Anthropology in Canada: Some Characteristics of the Disciplines and their Current University Programs.* Montreal, Canadian Sociology and Anthropology Association
Dawson, Carl A. 1934. *The Settlement of the Peace River Country.* Vol. VI of *Canadian Frontiers of Settlement.* Toronto, Macmillan Co
– 1936. *Group Settlement: Ethnic Communities in Western Canada.* Vol. VII of *Canadian Frontiers of Settlement.* Toronto, Macmillan Co

Dumont, Fernand. 1971. 'L'Etude systématique de la société globale canadienne-française,' *La Société canadienne-française*, M. Rioux and Y. Martin, eds. Montreal, Editions Hurtubise HMH. Pp.389-404 (first published in 1962)

Dumont, Fernand and Guy Rocher. 1971. 'Introduction à une sociologie du Canada français,' *La Société canadienne-française*, M. Rioux and Y. Martin, eds. Montreal, Editions Hurtubise HMH. Pp.189-207

Duncan, Otis Dudley. 1966. 'Path Analysis: Sociological Examples,' *American Journal of Sociology*, 72, pp.1-16

Easterbrook, W.T. and H.G.J. Aitken. 1956. *Canadian Economic History*. Toronto, Macmillan Co

Easterlin, Richard E. 1973. 'Does Money Buy Happiness?', *The Public Interest*, 30, pp.3-10

Eayrs, James. 1964. 'Sharing a Continent: The Hard Issues,' *The United States and Canada*, J.S. Dickey, ed. The American Assembly, Columbia University. Englewood Cliffs, NJ, Prentice-Hall. Pp.55-94

Elkin, Frederick. 1973. *Rebels and Colleagues: Advertising and Social Change in French Canada*. Montreal, McGill-Queen's University Press

Falardeau, Jean-C. 1960. *Roots and Values in Canadian Lives*. Toronto, University of Toronto Press

Garigue, Philippe. 1962. *La Vie familiale des canadiens-français*. Montreal, Presses de l'Université de Montréal

Germani, Gino. 1963. *Política y sociedad en una epoca de transición*. Buenos Aires, Editorial Paidos

Goffman, Erving. 1971. *Relations in Public: Microstudies of the Public Order*. New York, Basic Books

Goode, William J. 1964. *The Family*. Englewood Cliffs, NJ, Prentice-Hall

Goodman, Leo A. 1965. 'On the Statistical Analysis of Mobility Tables,' *American Journal of Sociology*, 70, pp.564-85

– 1972. 'A Model for the Analysis of Surveys,' *American Journal of Sociology*, 77, pp.1035-86

Gouldner, Alvin W. 1970. *The Coming Crisis of Western Sociology*. New York, Basic Books

Guindon, Hubert. 1967. 'Two Cultures: An Essay on Nationalism, Class, and Ethnic Tension,' *Contemporary Canada*, R.H. Leach, ed. Durham, NC, Duke University Press. Pp.33-59

Habermas, Jürgen. 1972. *Theorie und Praxis: Sozialphilosophische Studien*. Frankfurt, Suhrkamp

Hall, Oswald. 1948. 'The Stages of a Medical Career,' *American Journal of Sociology*, 53, pp.327-36

Hamilton, Richard F. 1973. Canada's Non-Farm Labour Force: Specifications and Trends.' Unpublished manuscript

Hauser, Philip M. 1964. 'Labour Force,' *Handbook of Modern Sociology*, R.E.L. Faris, ed. Chicago, Rand McNally. Pp. 160-90

– ed. 1969. *The Population Dilemma*. Second edition. The American Assembly, Columbia University. Englewood Cliffs, NJ, Prentice-Hall

Henripin, Jacques. 1971. 'De la fécondité naturelle à la prévention des naissances; l'évolution démographique au Canada depuis le XVIIe siècle, *'La Société canadienne-française*, M. Rioux and Y. Martin, eds. Montreal, Editions Hurtubise HMH. Pp.215-26
– 1972. *Trends and Factors of Fertility in Canada.* Ottawa, Dominion Bureau of Statistics
Hodgetts, A.B. 1968. *What Culture? What Heritage? A Study of Civic Education in Canada.* Toronto, Ontario Institute for Studies in Education
Homans, George C. 1950. *The Human Group.* New York, Harcourt Brace and Co
– 1964. 'Contemporary Theory in Sociology,' *Handbook of Modern Sociology*, R.E.L. Faris, ed. Chicago, Rand McNally. Pp.951-77
Hughes, Everett C. 1943. *French Canada in Transition.* Chicago, University of Chicago Press. (Paperback edition, 1963)
– 1958. *Men and Their Work.* Glencoe, Ill., Free Press
– 1969. 'The Sociological Enterprise in Canada.' Commencement Address, Queen's University, Kingston, Ontario. (Mimeographed)
– 1971. *The Sociological Eye.* Chicago, Aldine Publishing Co
Innis, Harold A. 1962. *The Fur Trade in Canada.* Toronto, University of Toronto Press
Janowitz, Morris. 1960. *The Professional Soldier: A Social and Political Portrait.* Glencoe, Ill., Free Press
– 1972. 'Professionalization of Sociology,' *American Journal of Sociology*, 78, pp.105-35
Jonassohn, Kurt, ed. 1972. *Urban Life Styles: Observations in Montreal – '72.* Montreal, Department of Sociology, Sir George Williams University
Jones, Frank E. 1961. 'The Socialization of the Infantry Recruit,' *Canadian Society: Sociological Perspectives*, B.R. Blishen et al., eds. Toronto, Macmillan Co. Pp. 285-98
Kalbach, Warren E. 1970. *The Impact of Immigration on Canada's Population.* Ottawa, Dominion Bureau of Statistics
Keyfitz, Nathan. 1968. *Introduction to the Mathematics of Population.* Reading, Mass., Addison-Wesley
König, René, ed. 1969. 'Aspekte der Entwicklungs Soziologie,' *Kölner Zeitschrift für Soziologie und Sozialpsychologie*, 13. (Special issue)
Kunkel, John H. 1970. *Society and Economic Growth: A Behavioral Inspection of Social Change.* New York, Oxford University Press
Lambert, Wallace B. 1955. 'Measurement of the Linguistic Dominance of Bilinguals,' *Journal of Abnormal and Social Psychology*, 50, pp.197-200
Lambert, Wallace B., J. Havelka and C. Crosby. 1958. 'The Influence of Language Acquisition Contexts on Bilingualism,' *Journal of Abnormal and Social Psychology*, 56, pp.239-44
Lefebvre, Henri. 1958. *Critique de la vie quotidienne.* Paris, L'Arche Editeur
Lipset, Seymour M. 1950. *Agrarian Socialism.* Berkeley, University of California Press

– 1960. *Political Man: The Social Bases of Politics.* New York, Doubleday
– 1968. 'Canada and the United States – A Comparative View,' *Canada: A Sociological Profile,* W.E. Mann, ed. Toronto, Copp Clark. Pp.488-98
Lynd, Robert S. and Helen Merrell Lynd. 1929. *Middletown: A Study in Modern American Culture.* New York, Harcourt, Brace and Co
Martin, Yves. 1971. 'Les études urbaines au Canada français,' *La Société canadienne-française,* M. Rioux and Y. Martin, eds. Montreal, Editions Hurtubise HMH. Pp.253-62
McDonald, Lynn. 1969. 'Religion and Voting: A Study of the 1968 Canadian Federal Election in Ontario,' *Canadian Review of Sociology and Anthropology,* 6, pp.129-61
McFarlane, Bruce A. 1965. *Dental Manpower in Canada.* Royal Commission on Health Services. Ottawa, the Queen's Printer
Meisel, John. 1967. 'Canadian Parties and Politics,' *Contemporary Canada,* Richard H. Leach, ed. Durham, NC, Duke University Press. Pp.124-47
Merton, Robert K. 1957. *Social Theory and Social Structure.* Revised edition. New York, Free Press, Collier-Macmillan
– 1972. 'Insiders and Outsiders: A Chapter in the Sociology of Knowledge,' *American Journal of Sociology,* 78, pp.9-47
Mills, C. Wright. 1959. *The Sociological Imagination.* New York, Oxford University Press
Naegele, Kaspar D. 1961. 'Canadian Society: Some Reflections,' *Canadian Society: Sociological Perspectives,* B.R. Blishen *et al.,* eds. Toronto, Macmillan Co. Pp.1-53
Nisbet, Robert A. 1966. *The Sociological Tradition.* New York, Basic Books
Oliver, Michael K. 1972. 'Ethnicity in Canadian Politics: French-English Relations.' Unpublished manuscript
Orkin, Mark M. 1970. *Speaking Canadian English.* Toronto, General Publishing Co
– 1971. *Speaking Canadian French.* Revised edition. Toronto, General Publishing Co
Ostry, Sylvia, ed. 1972. *Canadian Higher Education in the Seventies.* Ottawa, Information Canada
Parsons, Talcott. 1941. *The Structure of Social Action.* Glencoe, Ill., Free Press
– 1960. *Structure and Process in Modern Societies.* Glencoe, Ill., Free Press
– 1964. *Essays in Sociological Theory.* Revised edition. New York, Free Press, Collier-Macmillan
– 1970. 'On Building Social System Theory: A Personal History,' *Daedalus,* 99(Fall), pp.826-81
Petersen, William. 1955. *Planned Migration: The Social Determinants of the Dutch-Canadian Movement.* Berkeley, University of California Press
Porter, John. 1965. *Vertical Mosaic: An Analysis of Social Class and Power in Canada.* Toronto, University of Toronto Press
– 1967. 'Le Caractère canadien au XXème siècle,' *Revue de psychologie des peuples,* 3, pp.238-47

40 N. Keyfitz

- 1968. 'The Future of Upward Mobility,' *American Sociological Review*, 33, pp.5-15
- 1972. 'Some Questions about Ethnic Pluralism Asked from a Canadian Perspective.' Paper prepared for a conference on Ethnic Problems in the Contemporary World, American Academy of Arts and Science
Regenstreif, Peter. 1972. ' "Anti-Nationalism" in Canada: A Comment on Canadian Political Culture,' *ACSUS Newsletter*, 2:2, pp.6-12
Rioux, Marcel. 1969. 'Des colonisés peuvent-ils devenir des partenaires égaux?', *Sociologie et sociétés*, 1, pp.319-20
Ritsert, Jürgen. 1972. *Inhaltsanalyse und Ideologiekritik*. Frankfurt, Athënaum Verlag
Rocher, Guy. 1969. *Introduction à la sociologie générale*. Vol. 3. *Changement social et action historique*. Montreal, Editions HMH
- 1969. 'Le Canada: un pays à rebatir?', *Canadian Review of Sociology and Anthropology*, 6, pp.119-25
- 1972. 'Les Ambiguités d'un Canada bilingue et multiculturel.' Paper presented at the annual meeting of the Canadian Sociology and Anthropology Association
- 1972. *Talcott Parsons et la sociologie américaine*. Paris, Presses Universitaires de France
Ross, Aileen D. 1961. 'The Cultural Effects of Population Changes in the Eastern Townships,' *Canadian Society: Sociological Perspectives*, B.R. Blishen *et al.*, eds. Toronto, Macmillan Co. Pp.99-113
Ryder, Norman B. and Charles F. Westoff. 1971. *Reproduction in the United States 1965*. Princeton, Princeton University Press
Sartre, Jean-Paul. 1960. *Critique de la raison dialectique*, Vol. 1: *Théorie des ensembles pratiques*. Paris, Gallimard
Schwartz, Mildred A. 1968. 'Barriers to Consensus on Canadian Identity,' *Canada: A Sociological Profile*, W.E. Mann, ed. Toronto, Copp Clark. Pp.308-25
Seeley, John R., R.A. Sim and E.W. Loosley. 1956. *Crestwood Heights: A Study of the Culture of Suburban Life*. New York, Basic Books
Sévigny, Robert. 1971. *L'Expérience réligieuse chez les jeunes*. Montreal, Presses de l'Université de Montréal
Shils, Edward. 1961. *The Intellectual between Tradition and Modernity: The Indian Situation*. The Hague, Mouton & Co
Simon, Herbert. 1957. *Models of Man*. New York, John Wiley & Sons
Skolnick, Jerome H. 1966. *Justice without Trial: Law Enforcement in Democratic Society*. New York, John Wiley & Sons
Solomon, David N. 1961. 'Sociological Research in a Military Organization,' *Canadian Society: Sociological Perspectives*, B.R. Blishen *et al.*, eds. Toronto, Macmillan Co. Pp.275-85
- 1968. 'The Soldierly Self and the Peace-Keeping Role: Canadian Officers in Peace-Keeping Forces,' *Military Profession and Military Regimes*, Jacques van Doorn, ed. The Hague, Mouton & Co. Pp.52-69
Sorokin, Pitirim A. 1964. *Social and Cultural Mobility*. New York, Free Press, Collier-Macmillan

Spicer, Keith. 1966. *A Samaritan State? External Aid in Canada's Foreign Policy.*
Toronto, University of Toronto Press
Statistical Abstract of the United States 1972. Ninety-third annual edition. Washington, DC, United States Bureau of the Census
Steeves, Allan D. 1971. *A Complete Bibliography in Sociology and a Partial Bibliography in Anthropology of MA Theses and PhD Dissertations Completed at Canadian Universities up to 1970.* Ottawa, Department of Sociology and Anthropology, Carleton University
Stone, Leroy O. 1969. *Migration in Canada: Some Regional Aspects.* Ottawa, Dominion Bureau of Statistics
Stone, Philip J. 1966. *The General Inquirer: A Computer Approach to Content Analysis.* Cambridge, Mass, MIT Press
Westley, William A. 1953. 'Violence and the Police,' *American Journal of Sociology*, 59, pp.34-41
Westley, William A. and Margaret Westley. 1971. *The Emerging Worker.* Montreal, McGill-Queen's University Press
White, Harrison C. 1962. *An Anatomy of Kinship: Mathematical Models for Structures of Cumulated Roles.* Englewood Cliffs, NJ, Prentice-Hall
– 1970. *Chains of Opportunity: System Models of Mobility in Organizations.* Cambridge, Mass., Harvard University Press
Whyte, Don. 1973. 'Canadian Identity and the Colonial Tradition.' Unpublished manuscript
Wrong, Dennis H. 1961. 'The Oversocialized Conception of Man in Modern Sociology,' *American Sociological Review*, 26, pp.183-93
Zakuta, Leo. 1970. 'On "Filthy Lucre," ' *Human Nature and Collective Behavior: Papers in Honor of Herbert Blumer*, T. Shibutani, ed. Englewood Cliffs, NJ, Prentice-Hall. Pp.260-70

Commentary J. FREEDMAN

Although Professor Keyfitz's paper deals with many issues, his remarks about how sociology has applied itself to social problems are especially illuminating.* Throughout these comments runs a common thread: this is, that the complexity of social issues cannot be appreciated by their appearances. Healing, as he so appropriately puts it, cannot be wholly understood in terms of available technical descriptions of disease. Likewise, an appreciation of the dynamics of social issues is

* Occasionally these comments refer to a somewhat different, earlier version of this paper.

considerably complicated when one considers prejudices, habits and attitudes, all of which make up the awareness people have of their social surroundings.

The lesson here is that social problems are inscrutable. And this inscrutability is not a mirage that can be dispelled by common sense. The obvious solution is seldom the correct one. The correct answers depend on an intimate understanding of the configuration of the forces which constitute a social situation. Any description of a stable society must describe this configuration. Any directed change must reckon with it. These forces make up the unknowns which social research attempts to unearth.

With what procedure – that is, with what method and what philosophical orientation – is one best equipped to go about discovering these unknowns in any given area of the world? In particular, how does one go about approaching the question: what is it which renders Canadian identity unique? A major thrust of Professor Keyfitz's paper, and one of his major contributions in the social sciences, has been to describe quantitatively the social conditions for the directions that present society is going in, or seeks to go in. He has made mention of some very recent research (though not necessarily his own) in this vein: a study of the correlation between income and generalized happiness; a study relating parents' income to their children's likelihood of attending college.

In each of these problems, one is searching for the relevant variables and arranging them appropriately, aiming to get just below the logical ceiling, that is, the last word in causality: to capture all variables so that their dependence on external phenomena and their interdependence with other relevant variables, is under control. At this point causal inference can be made.

The attractiveness of this procedure is that it has cast the variables into a formal mould. Undoubtedly, this is of considerable value. One wonders, however, on what basis, according to what procedure, these variables have been selected. By what procedure was income thought to be relevant to happiness? How has the problem been phrased in the first place?

When a sociologist works in his own society he may rely, only with caution, on an awareness of his own social environment. When he concerns himself with societies alien to his own, as anthropologists have a tradition of doing, then such an awareness is of little use. Happiness in East Africa has to do, at least partially, with the proximity of one's land to a dependable water source. Having once established this tenet, one then may go on to quantify the notion of happiness, perhaps in terms of feet or kilometers. Yet the fact remains and should be forcefully put: the arrangement of variables for a sociological description is first of all the product of sensitivity and intuition, brought to bear in a first-hand experience of the problem; and secondly the application of formal skills of analysis. This is largely why field work – that uniquely anthropological contribution to the social sciences – has remained such an important part of the practice, if not the theory of the discipline.

But this field-work experience, in which intuition plays such a major role, is far from Professor Keyfitz's description of the role of empirical research in sociology. Empirical research, as he has described it, mainly serves two purposes of verification. It is a kind of postscript to the research project: the gathering of those data called for specifically by hypotheses formulated in advance.

If I can add anything to Professor Keyfitz's paper, it is an anthropological perspective toward empirical research. When work in the field is thought of as a foreword as well as a postscript to research one is inclined not only to gather data but also to experience the milieu in which the data are sought. Ideally, the milieu itself will suggest the issues of most urgent concern to the social scientist. The lesson that such a perspective relies upon may be phrased as a paradox: the only guarantee of an objective description – and by this one means biased by neither popular nor scientific preconceptions – involves in the first moments of research, a thoroughly subjective experience. It is only in this way that the variables selected are assured of being relevant to the problem.

There is another advantage to anthropology's almost obsessive concern not to misconstrue the sentiments, attitudes and habits of the people under investigation. It seeks to render a description which reveals, above all else, the uniqueness of the object society. Many anthropologists follow this procedure, even at some cost to the search for rules of social organization which are invariable cross-culturally. This brings me to a final point – one which bears directly on the application of social sciences to the specific interests of Canadian society — the description of a national character.

It was largely in view of this concern to describe the uniqueness of cultures that anthropologists were chosen during and after the Second World War to commit their efforts to studying the idea of national character and national morale. This was partially motivated by the American government's desire to know how to increase morale by playing upon the elements of national *esprit de corps.* A number of interesting papers appeared on this issue of national character, perhaps the most interesting of which was written by Gregory Bateson.

There have been a number of arguments against the feasibility of describing such a thing as national character, most of them claiming that there is not sufficient uniformity within national boundaries to warrant the effort. These arguments emphasize the degree of subcultural differentiation, the extreme heterogeneity of cultural norms, the considerable amount of deviance in modern societies, and so on. But for Bateson, this heterogeneity is not a problem. In fact, it provides the very clue to describing some of the unique regularities which govern the behaviour of members of a national community.

His argument, briefly, is this: it is indeed difficult to isolate values which are uniformly held by the citizenry of a single country. The interaction of individuals such as parent and child, or of interest groups such as government and public, partakes of divergent values. The children act with submission and the parents with dominance. The government assumes an attitude toward the public which is distinct from the attitude the public maintains in dealing with the government. The way that individuals in interaction, and the way that groups in interaction, differentiate themselves is what, in part, produces the heterogeneity of a society.

But these various modes of differentiating between elements of the society obey, he observes, recognizable regularities. The heterogeneity within national communities poses no particular problem since the rules which generate this heterogeneity are, in themselves, the most regular features of the culture. According to Bateson, these regularities which describe rules for differentiation also serve to account for what is unique about a national community. He has demonstrated, as an example, a striking difference between the parent-child relationship in England and in America. In England the parent customarily plays the role of exhibitionist – a prerogative associated presumably with the exercise of authority – while the child remains a spectator. The continuum of spectator-exhibitionis is reversed within American families, in which the child customarily takes on an exhibitionist role, while the parents play the spectator. The relative absence of parental authority, unique to American families, becomes particularly clear when cast in terms of rules for differentiation between parent and child.

Bateson's proposals for the study of a national character are, I think, worthy of Professor Keyfitz's claim that sociologists are able to surprise those who rely upon appearances and common sense. His findings are evidence of the fact that sociological descriptions are capable of discerning regularities that appearances conceal.

His insights, furthermore, are inspired by an overriding concern, which I have made some effort to underscore as uniquely anthropological: to describe social facts in a manner that most successfully demonstrates the uniqueness of the specific culture in which they are observed.

As I reflect upon these comments, and re-read Professor Keyfitz's paper, I am impressed that I have not really said anything that he has not, in some way, touched upon. His comprehensiveness is evidence of his erudition. What I have done, hopefully, is to describe, with reference to the issues of empirical research and the subject of national character, how anthropology can contribute, in conjunction with sociology, to the laudable enterprise Professor Keyfitz has outlined.

Commentary M. ROKEACH

In the brief amount of time allotted to me, it is, of course, not possible to comment exhaustively on all the issues and themes that are touched upon in Nathan Keyfitz's scholarly and comprehensive essay. Instead, I can only respond very selectively to just a few of his major themes, and my comments will overlap somewhat with those that have just been made by Professor Freedman. What interested me most was what Professor Keyfitz has had to say about the distinctiveness of Canadian culture, whether a distinctive Canadian sociology is possible or desirable and, finally, the problem of fragmentation in sociology. Most of the comments I now propose to make are intended to reinforce and elaborate on what Professor Keyfitz has said and others are intended to offer some alternative viewpoints.

CANADIAN DISTINCTIVENESS

Both Professor Keyfitz and I have attempted to address ourselves to the question of what it means to be a Canadian, and especially to the question of how Canadians can be said to differ from others, particularly Americans. I cannot tell from a reading of Professor Keyfitz's paper whether we agree or disagree on the subject of Canadian distinctiveness. On the one hand, Professor Keyfitz suggests that on the whole Canadians are rather similar to Englishmen and Americans, and that he does not see all that much difference among them. On the other hand, Professor Keyfitz offers some observations suggesting that there may after all be some important differences in the cultural perspectives of Canadians and Americans. 1/He observes that Canada can but chooses not to use its power of occasionally invading a South-American country. I suppose he mentions this in order to point out that this is in contrast to the way Americans are prone to behave. I suppose, too, that Professor Keyfitz is trying to draw our attention to an important difference between Canadians and Americans. 2/In contrast to American socialization practices, Professor Keyfitz tells us, children in Canada are not imprinted with the symbols of nationalism in the same unambiguous, unequivocal way as children in America are. So I end up not being sure whether Professor Keyfitz feels that Canadians are distinctive or not distinctive.

Whenever we go to another country, whether it is to visit Canada or England or wherever, the first thing we are on the alert for are the differences. I remember when I came to the University of Western Ontario, people were continually asking me whether I had noticed any differences yet between Canadians and Americans. I would usually answer, somewhat uncertainly, in the affirmative, and I would quickly add that I was not sure how to describe these differences. I suppose that most of us who have travelled abroad have experienced the cultural differences but can't quite put a finger on them. This whole question is really an empirical matter which is researchable. It is time that we moved beyond anecdotal, journalistic accounts to the quantitative measurement of differences — this, I believe, is one of the major contributions that social science has to offer that goes beyond good journalism.

In this connection, I would like to cite a recent study which was drawn to my attention by my good friend and colleague, Neil Vidmar, a study done by Arnold, White and Tigert of the Faculty of Management Studies at the University of Toronto. Using attitudinal data collected from national samples tested in Canada and the United States in 1969 and 1970 they summarize their findings, too long to present here, as follows: they find that Canadians are 'less independent, less competitive, less self-confident, and less innovative than Americans. In addition, they are more prepared to accept government control but are less likely to exert leadership or use credit.' These are Canadians talking about Canadians. Their findings seem, on the whole, consistent with the kind of data that I presented but I'm not sure whether they are consistent with the kind of data presented by Professor Keyfitz, for the reason that I have already indicated. I would like to draw attention, however, to one interpretation by these authors which I would want to take issue with. Whereas they would conclude from their data that Canadians are more prepared than Americans to accept government controls, I would prefer to conclude from the same data that Canadians are on the whole somewhat more egalitarian than Americans in their orientation and are therefore more prepared than Americans to endorse and support social-welfare legislation (which Arnold, White and Tigert call government control), which would reduce the gaps between the more and the less privileged in Canadian society. In other words, there is all the world of difference between being in favour of government control that would perpetuate a privileged position in society and being in favour of government control that is designed to prevent the perpetuation of such privileges.

Professor Keyfitz goes on to point to some differences between the French-Canadian and English-Canadian culture. He feels that the present French-Canadian culture is diverging more or less from French culture and also from English-Canadian culture and, moreover, that this French-Canadian cultural independence is being reflected in its sociology. In his closing paragraph on this issue, Professor Keyfitz says: 'In conversation, some Ontario sociologists have expressed envy of Quebec; when there comes to be an autonomous and unified English-Canadian society, they say, some degree of autonomy will be possible for English Canadian sociology.' I think it is safe to assume that this view that Professor Keyfitz attributes to 'some Ontario sociologists' is also his own view. We need to carry out intensive and concerted empirical research to determine more systematically the exact differences and similarities in the values of French and English Canadians, whether or not it is indeed the case, as Professor Keyfitz suggests, that the French Canadians are diverging more from the French in recent years and, if so, in exactly what way. To reiterate and elaborate on a point that I made in my own paper, we need more detailed research on the precise similarities and differences which may exist between French Canadians and English Canadians (and while we are on the subject, comparative studies should also include Canadian Indians, Eskimos, Ukranians, Italians, and all the other peoples that are now identifying themselves as Canadians). And we need more empirical research that would plot the cultural convergences and divergences which may be taking place.

CANADIAN SOCIOLOGY

Again, I cannot decide, after reading Professor Keyfitz's paper, whether he is advocating or arguing against the desirability of a distinctive and autonomous Canadian sociology. On the one hand, Professor Keyfitz seems to be chiding Canadian sociology because its 'subjects of investigation have been similar to those of the United States. This is an opportunity lost in so far as Canadian society has distinctive features and problems which should instigate new and important work.' 'Why,' Professor Keyfitz goes on to ask, 'has Canadian sociology not gone further along lines special to itself?' Professor Keyfitz then goes on to discuss five distinctively or potentially distinctively Canadian problems 'in order to demonstrate that there is a potential Canadian sociology ... capable of inspiring creative research ... whether by Canadian-born, American-born, British-born, or other scholars.'

On the other hand, Professor Keyfitz goes on to say later in his essay, 'Whether there can be a Canadian sociology is a thorny question not to be answered by a simple yes or no.' He speaks of two models which sociology might follow: the continental model and the nationalistic model.

In a similar vein, Professor Keyfitz observes on the one hand that Canadian sociology is too much like American sociology, and that unlike American, British, German, and French sociology, it is not taking at least some of its problems from 'national concerns'. On the other hand, Professor Keyfitz observes: 'Of course a discipline does not take its subjects of research from the public, but rather from its own internal development. Scholars tackle problems arising out of the research of other scholars.'

So I again end up not knowing where Professor Keyfitz stands on the issue of an independent Canadian sociology. A logician might say that Professor Keyfitz is inconsistent in his views on a distinctively Canadian sociology. But as a psychologist, I would prefer to conclude that Professor Keyfitz is merely ambivalent about it. That is, he has mixed feelings about it, on the one hand genuinely seeking to encourage an autonomous and nationally distinctive Canadian sociology, and on the other hand, doubting its desirability, on grounds of a more continental rather than nationalistic perspective about scientific knowledge.

I have already stated my own position on this issue. I doubt that there can be a Canadian sociology (or psychology or economics, etc.) for the same reason that I doubt that there can be a distinctively Bulgarian sociology. It may well be true that British sociology has, as Professor Keyfitz points out, a distinctive philosophical tinge, that Germany's critical sociology is distinctively historical, ideological, and philosophical, and that French sociology is distinctively logical and general in its orientation. But such distinctiveness seems to be a function not so much of 'national concerns' as of history and tradition. In the final analysis, I believe that a more fruitful question is now how distinctive or autonomous Canadian sociology (or whatever) ought to be but rather how good it ought to be. I fear that an over-concern with nationalistic distinctiveness and autonomy is something of a red herring that can all too easily divert our attention away from a more pertinent and salient concern with the quality of academic life, which, of course, knows no national boundaries.

FRAGMENTATION

Both Professor Keyfitz and I deplore the fragmentation that each of us sees in our respective disciplines. I wish once again to broaden the discussion to point not only to the intradisciplinary fragmentation but also to the interdisciplinary fragmentation. All the social sciences can be said to have the same purpose; they are all concerned, in the final analysis, with the question of antecedents and consequents of social behaviour. Psychologists no less than sociologists, sociologists no less than historians, historians no less than anthropologists, and anthropologists no less than political scientists have, for example, been more or less equally concerned with problems of war and peace, aggression and altruism, and competition and cooperation and with the problem of autonomy versus domination. They are all to one extent or another concerned with the alleviation of such social problems as prejudice and discrimination, conflict and violence, deviance and alienation, and the generation gap. But there is a fragmentation of knowledge across the social science disciplines, even when the substantive interests are identical, and I would attribute all such fragmentation within and between disciplines to differences in preference for theoretical or analytical perspectives as well as to differences in preference for method. Whatever their causes it can be described in Freudian terms as a function of compartmentalization and perhaps repression, and in Lewinian terms as a function of a structural rigidity and lack of communication across boundaries. I thus close in the hope that the Social Science Centre at this university, in this new home, will be sensitive to this problem which Professor Keyfitz regards as the greatest ailment of sociology and which I would regard also and more generally as the greatest ailment of the social sciences.

REFERENCES

Arnold, S.J., J.S. White and D.J. Tigert. 1972. 'Canadians and Americans: A Comparative Analysis,' Working Paper Series, Faculty of Management Studies, University of Toronto

Gans, H.J. 1968. 'Culture and Class in the Study of Poverty: An Approach to Antipoverty Research,' *On Understanding Poverty*, Daniel P. Moynihan, ed. New York, Basic Books

Lewis, O. 1966. *La Vida: A Puerto Rican Family in the Culture of Poverty – San Juan and New York.* New York, Random House

Moynihan, D.P. 1967. 'The Moynihan Report and its Critics,' *Commentary*, 43, pp.31-45

Parker, S. and R.J. Kleiner. 1970. 'The Culture of Poverty: An Adjustive Dimension,' *American Anthropologist*, 72, pp.516-27

Rainwater, L. 1968. 'The Problem of Lower Class Culture and Poverty-War Strategy,' *On Understanding Poverty*, Daniel P. Moynihan, ed. New York, Basic Books

Rokeach, M. and S. Parker. 1970. 'Values as Social Indicators of Poverty and Race Relations in America,' *The Annals of the American Academy of Political and Social Science*, 388, pp.97-111

C.B. MACPHERSON

2
After strange gods:
Canadian political science 1973

I am not generally accounted a great admirer of Edmund Burke, but
when I am asked to discourse on the subject given me here, I must
admit to some sympathy with Burke's stand on the matter of constantly digging up the roots. Castigating the admirers of the French
Revolution, in 1790, he asserted: 'It has been the misfortune, not as
these gentlemen think it, the glory, of this age, that everything is to be
discussed; as if the constitution of our country were to be always a
subject rather of altercation than enjoyment.'[1] Substitute 'our
discipline' for Burke's 'our country' and I am greatly tempted to agree.
Burke went on: 'For this reason, as well as for the satisfaction of those
among you (if any such you have among you) who may wish to profit
of examples, I venture to trouble you with a few thoughts upon each of
these establishments.'

The establishments he referred to were 'an established church, an
established monarchy, an established aristocracy, and an established
democracy, each in the degree it exists, and in no greater.' I hesitate to
suggest modern parallels in the Canadian political science establishment: I must leave each of you to speculate about that. Perhaps the
image of an established church is closer to our situation than the
curious thing Burke meant by 'an established democracy' (which was in
fact the voting power of 400,000 people out of a population some
twenty times as large).

There can be no doubt that there is an establishment in Canadian political science. It is difficult to see how it could be otherwise. The organization of the profession ensures it. Consider the extent to which tenure committees, editors of academic journals and academic book publishers, and the bodies which distribute grants for research and publication and for that proto-publication we call sabbatical leave, rely for advice on the established members of the profession, not necessarily the most senior but those who are already respected. To whom else can they turn but the acknowledged professionals who have established themselves, by their achievements similarly judged some years earlier? How else could a university press, or a learned journal, or the Canada Council, or the Social Science Research Council, operate? No other way. But this does establish an establishment.

What has the establishment done, and what is it doing? A case can be made for not asking such questions. The case is Burke's: don't try to pull everything up by the roots every few years. If we subscribe to that, there is no excuse for another enquiry, in 1973, into the position and prospects of Canadian political science. For the roots have been pulled up for examination often enough, and recently enough. The first pull was in 1889, when Bourinot presented a paper to the Royal Society of Canada on 'The Study of Political Science in Canadian Universities'.[2] The next, so far as I can find, was an article fifty years later, in 1938, 'On the Study of Politics in Canada'.[3] There was another one in 1942,[4] three more in 1950-1,[5] another in 1957[6] and two more in 1967.[7] Since I wrote four of these nine assessments, beginning with the 1938 one, I may be forgiven some distaste for doing yet another, and forgiven for wondering how much more digging up of the roots is useful or justified. Shouldn't we all just be *doing* political science, instead of talking and writing about how it has been done, is being done, and (worst of all) should be done, let alone how it has been *taught*, is being taught, and should be taught?

The answer, I think, is that we *should* just be doing political science, and teaching it, unless there is some reason to think that what we are doing is misdirected, or faulty in some remediable ways, or falling short in quality or quantity of what might reasonably be expected of us. Since there are usually some authorities, both within the discipline and in sister disciplines, telling us that much of our work and teaching is misdirected or faulty (and never has this been more so than in the last two decades), there is a *prima facie* case that something is wrong. And of course the only way of finding whether this justifies a new investigation is to make a new investigation.

The charges and counter-charges in recent decades have been about, and have come from within, the whole European, English and American profession. Doubt about the direction political science is taking, and certainty about its taking the wrong course, is largely a North-Atlantic phenomenon. That is to be expected, for the bulk of political science is done in the countries bordering on the North Atlantic. Much of the disquiet, of course, has arisen out of the so-called behavioural revolution and reactions to it. The carping, the claiming and disclaiming, are not as evident in Canadian thinking as elsewhere. Some Canadian political scientists have taken an active part in it,[8] but as contributors to the general debate, not as critics or upholders of trends in Canada. Canadians on the whole have been rather uncritical of each other. Our surveys of our own profession have tended to mark achievements, and sometimes (as in the surveys made in the early 1950s) to deplore the slow rate of growth. Growth has been rapid since the fifties; perhaps the vast amount to record has made assessment of trends and of quality seem less urgent.

I do not intend here to go over the ground covered in the papers already cited. The origins and early years of Canadian political science are now well enough known. And the strides made down to 1967 are ably set out in the two papers produced that year. Professor Smiley's paper, devoted mainly to the major contributions to Canadian political science since 1945, goes into considerable detail. He finds that most of the contributions can be brought under three headings: 'studies of parties and voting behaviour, studies of the political relations between English- and French-speaking Canadians, and interpretive studies of the Canadian political system as such';[9] apart from these he finds significant work on particular public policies (for example, immigration, combines legislation, regional resource development, defence) and on public policy devices and processes (for example, public corporations, royal commissions, parliamentary control of public expenditures, the ombudsman, federal grants-in-aid to the provinces). Amid his conspectus of all this work, he draws attention to lacunae: little or nothing on the politics of the House of Commons, on the government and politics of the largest provinces, on the office of the prime minister and the provincial premiers, and on the two largest parties, and little examination of assumptions about the Canadian political system as a whole, which are too readily taken over from extra-Canadian work or from other Canadian disciplines. All of this survey and assessment is so well done that I would not attempt, even if I were competent, to redo it.

The five or six years since his survey is rather too short a period to discern significant differences in the main lines he has depicted – at least I haven't discerned enough to justify a quinquennial addendum. A few of the lacunae have been filled (one notably by F.F. Schindeler's study of Ontario government[10]) but the main lines of the Smiley survey do not seem to me to stand in need of any substantial amendment.

Yet there is more to be said. For one thing, looking over all the surveys of the last thirty-five years, one may detect a curious blindness in most of them. I shall describe it, in terms of the most recent survey (Smiley's), as the lacuna in the lacunae. For another, there have been made available, in 1971, some new hard and soft data about the quantitative growth of Canadian political science, and the distribution of research interests and publication among the various fields cultivated by Canadian political scientists. Not the least interesting feature of this new material is the classification of fields which was employed. Let me first examine the implications of the new material, then go on to comment on the question of the lacunae.

The new data were elicited by the Canadian Political Science Association (CPSA), which decided, shortly after its divorce from the economists, to set up, jointly with the Société Canadienne de Science Politique, a Survey Committee to gather data on the Canadian political science profession, with a view to producing both a classified directory of the profession and an analysis of its publications and research interests and needs. The committee, chaired by Professor W.H.N. Hull, sent out a fairly elaborate mail questionnaire between October 1970 and February 1971. Some of its results have been reported in the *Directory of Political Scientists in Canada, 1970-71*, and in a paper, 'Political Science in Canada: A Profile', given by Professor Hull at the CPSA meeting in St John's in June 1971, with supporting documents.[11]

The Association also undertook an inquiry into Canadian graduate theses in political science, and has produced both a cumulative listing of all theses (for the MA and the PhD) from 1919 to 1970, and the first issue of an annual supplement listing theses in preparation in 1971-2. From this material some interesting conclusions can be drawn about both the growth of the profession and its range of interests.

Two measures of the numerical growth of Canadian political science are afforded. One is given by the number of political scientists teaching in Canadian universities. This is reported to be 664 in 1972-3. We have only to compare this number with the numbers reported at several earlier dates to see the growth: the figures may not be strictly comparable, but the orders of magnitude are clear. In 1950-1, the number reported was about 30,[12] in 1964-5, between 184 and 200,[13] in 1966-7, over 250.[14] In 1970-1, the figure stood at 517,[15] and in 1972-3, 664.[16] This growth rate is, by all indications of the rate of Canadian university expansion, past its peak.

The other measure of growth can be got from the listing of PhD theses in *Theses in Canadian Political Science* which reports (a) theses completed in the period 1919-70, (b) theses in progress, 1970, and (in the first annual supplement) (c) theses in progress, 1971-2. These theses are named and listed by fields. The numbers are not totalled. But a count in two of the main fields, 'Canadian Political Parties and Electoral Studies' and 'Political Philosophy', shows in each field almost exactly the same number of PhD theses in progress in 1971-2 as were completed in the whole fifty-two years from 1919 through 1970.[17]

The CPSA material also affords some measure of the distribution of current research interests and publications among fields within the Canadian political science profession in 1970. It is based on replies to a questionnaire asking each respondent to list up to two publications and to indicate in which of eight categories and sixty-four subcategories his or her current research should be placed. The material is of limited value because, although the rate of response to the questionnaire was high (77 per cent of the academic recipients), the limit on reporting of publications to two for each respondent leaves out a great many, which may skew the distribution; also, no difference in weight is given to articles and books. Nor, of course, was there any way of weighting the seriousness or the size of the research projects reported.

The figures are nonetheless of some interest. As one would expect, the largest of the eight fields, both in current research and in publications, was Canadian politics (institutions, processes and behaviour). But, somewhat surprisingly, it exceeded the next largest (foreign and cross-national political institutions and behaviour) by only a very slight margin: in research projects, Canadian politics 27 per cent, foreign and cross-national 25 per cent; in publications 30 per cent and 29 per cent. There is then a substantial gap, with international affairs and public policy having about 10 per cent each, political theory about 8 per cent, and the other three fields ranging down from 8 per cent to 1 per cent.

Two comments may be made about these figures. One concerns the classification of fields and subfields used in the questionnaire and in the *Directory of Political Scientists in Canada.*[18] The first thing that would strike anyone familiar with the earlier surveys of political science in Canada is how elaborate the classification is. Twenty years earlier it would have been sufficient to categorize the output of Canadian work under as few as five heads – say, Canadian government, comparative government, public administration, international relations, and political theory – and very few subheads would have been required. Now we have a classification under eight heads and sixty-four subheads; and all but two of the subheads (computer techniques and experimental design) are used, that is, have been listed by some members of the profession as one of their professional interests.

This may be taken – with a grain of salt, since it is possible that the questionnaire was more sophisticated than some of the respondents – as an indication of the distance Canadian political science has moved in the last two decades. At any rate it is safe to say that such a complex classification would have been meaningless in such a questionnaire twenty years ago. Few then would have thought of themselves as specialists in many of the subjects (or even recognized them as subjects) which are now given separate names, for instance, decision-making processes, mass participation and communications, political development and modernization, model building, survey design and analysis, political socialization, organization theory and behaviour, systems analysis. If this is evidence of the increasing range and sophistication of the political science practised in Canada, it also suggests an extensive Americanization, about which I shall make a further comment later.[19]

The other comment to be made on this material about the distribution between the various fields of political science is that it does not pretend to assess the worth of any of the work as contributions to the discipline of political science. The analysis of current research projects aggregates with equal weights 'projects' which are clearly significant and 'projects' scarcely begun and of unknown value. And as already noted, the analysis of published work, besides leaving some of it out, aggregates with equal weights short pieces which may be of slight significance and substantial books of recognized value.

Now it is difficult indeed to specify what constitutes a contribution to the discipline, or what are reasonable criteria of original work. One set of criteria which seems reasonable has been suggested by a recent writer:

In ascending order of rarity and acclaim, 'original work' is:
1/ the application of usual methods to some untouched tract of their usual subject matter;
2/ the correction of earlier work;
3/ the successful application of old methods to novel material;
4/ the improvement or invention of the methods themselves.

The writer adds:

The best work often does a bit of all of these. If its methodological invention is remarkable enough it may even found new disciplines or split or reunite old ones.[20]

One might restate the criterion of the top class by having it comprise works which have so transformed the field or subfield that no one subsequently can see things in it in the old way or can attempt to explain things in it without attending to the new framework (if only to try to refute it). We need not be too concerned about the top class, for its members will always be rare: we cannot all be a Marx or a Namier or a Keynes. We can, though, all aspire to one of the first three degrees of originality, and our contribution to the discipline may properly be judged on that basis.

Yet who is to judge? In fact, as the profession is organized, the judges are editors of and referees for journals and book publishers; book reviewers; and perhaps organizers of academic round tables, congresses, and association meetings. If we are concerned with Canadian contributions to the discipline of political science, and not just with contributions to Canadian political science, the most reliable judgment would appear to be international recognition by the same sort of judges. To insist on this, however, would be to handicap those whose work is entirely in the field of Canadian politics, for the scholar who writes about the government and politics of his own country cannot expect to get as much attention internationally as one whose field is, say, political theory or international affairs or cross-national or Third World politics. His work may be as original, by any of the criteria set out above, as the work of a colleague in history of thought or comparative communism, but it simply will not be as much noticed outside.

I do not see how this handicap could be offset except by leaving Canadian work on Canadian subject-matter to be judged by Canadians, while requiring international judgment of Canadian work on all other subject-matter. That course would have its dangers, although perhaps the Canadian political science community is now large enough and sure enough of itself for its members not to be afraid of wounding each other where thorough critical judgment entails wounding. A conventional adoption of a double judiciary might lead to acceptance of a double standard, which would be unfair in the other direction. But to draw back, for fear of that, from accepting international judgment of Canadian work on non-Canadian subjects would be taken as an announcement that we were not ready to meet standards accepted elsewhere. So we should probably settle for the double judiciary.

I have raised this question of standards and quality – of what constitutes a contribution to the discipline of political science – in the particular context of commenting on the limitations of the CPSA survey. For understandable reasons, that survey could not attempt to judge quality. But the problem of judging quality goes deeper. For I think no one of us could attempt to make such a judgment of the whole output of the discipline, if only because it is so wide-ranging. I certainly do not feel competent to do so, though I shall of course offer some remarks later which may sound like such a judgment.

But in the one field I am most familiar with, that of political theory (in the broad sense used in the CPSA classification, including general empirical theory, normative theory and history of theory), I think I can detect in the CPSA distribution figures a significant underestimate of the size of the Canadian contribution in relation to the size of the contribution in the other fields. The survey of publications by Canadian political scientists shows political theory as accounting for only 8 per cent of them (in comparison with 30 per cent for Canadian politics and 29 per cent for foreign and cross-national politics). I do not doubt that this is an accurate calculation of the data provided by the respondents to the questionnaire. But it would be easy to compile a list of a dozen books in political theory, by currently productive political scientists in Canadian universities, which have been internationally recognized as serious original works, some of them even in the top class of origin-ality.[21] I think it doubtful that a similar list of significant books by current Canadian scholars in the fields of either Canadian politics or foreign and cross-national politics, as judged by the double judiciary, would be three and a half times as long. I mention this not to suggest, as a political theorist myself, that there is nothing like leather, but to suggest that there may be a gap between quantitative findings and quantitative-qualitative findings.

Let me revert now to the Smiley assessment of 1967, to which I have already paid tribute; one feature deserves further notice. The survey was first given as a paper to a joint meeting of the newly-separated Canadian Political Science Association and Canadian Economics Association in June 1967. At the same meeting a similar paper was given by Professor Harry Johnson on the position of Canadian economics. But there was a striking difference between the two papers. Professor Smiley's was entitled 'Contributions to Canadian Political Science since the Second World War'; Professor Johnson's was entitled 'Canadian Contributions to the Discipline of Economics since the War'.[22] The difference in titles accurately indicated the difference in approach and content. Professor Johnson was assessing Canadian contributions to an international corpus of economics; Professor Smiley was assessing Canadian contributions to the study of Canadian politics. The difference is significant. The economist took for granted that international standards were to apply to Canadian work, that it should be judged on its worth as a contribution to a recognized body of economic theory. The political scientist took for granted that the Canadian work that mattered was Canadian contributions to the understanding of Canadian political phenomena. There is no reference in the Smiley assessment to Canadian work in any fields other than Canadian government and politics, unless one counts as an exception his reference to Corry's *Democratic Government and Politics* (1947), which of course is only partly about the Canadian system and does relate it, and the British and American systems, to questions of democratic and liberal values; presumably it is because of its Canadian content that it is cited as a Canadian contribution.[23] Smiley's omission of any Canadian work in non-Canadian fields is the lacuna in the lacunae to which I referred earlier. Moreover, his concluding remark, from which I must dissent, indicates that he was quite content with this basis of valuation: 'our credentials as a vital and important academic discipline must rest on our accomplishments in published scholarship on Canadian political structures and processes.'[24]

One is tempted to speculate on the reason for the difference between the economist's and the political scientist's approach. The most probable reason has to do with the difference in stature, by which I mean theoretical wholeness, between the two disciplines in general, that is, as world-wide or North Atlantic bodies of knowledge. The economist was able to assume that there was a recognized body of theory in relation to which new work anywhere was to be assessed, whether the content of the new work was refinement, or modification, or application, of the prevailing theory. The political scientist was not able to assume this, for the simple reason that in political science no such theory exists. Political science anywhere, not just in Canada, is not at a stage where everything relates in some clear or assignable way to a well-developed and widely accepted general theory. Political science is not, therefore, in a position to assess all new work automatically or primarily as application or modification of such theory.

It is true that one can point to the prevalence, in North Atlantic political science, of a more or less vague pluralist equilibrium model of the democratic system, but its prevalence is half-unconscious, and, partly because of this, it is under severe attack. It is true also that large claims are made for the need to develop a systematic framework for all political analysis. The claim is that we need to have one, not that we have one; and attempts to construct one have been at such a high level of abstraction that they are remote from and largely unusable by political scientists in any field. There is as yet no general or unifying theory worth much. This has recently (1971) been emphasized by David Easton, himself for the last two decades the leading North-Atlantic advocate of the importance of a systematic general theory.

Today we are still very far from anything that looks like a general theory. All that parades as political theory is in reality only the first small step on the way to the construction of theory. It consists largely of the formulation of theoretical frameworks of analysis and conceptual structures, not broadly integrated statements about the relationships of variables. Not only are we at a very early stage in theory construction but even within these limits no single paradigm has been widely accepted as most useful, however prevalent systems formulations may be. The selection of a theoretical approach is still very much an open matter, a characteristic of an 'immature' science.[25]

Given that political science in general is immature, it is not surprising that leading Canadian political scientists find no clear theory to relate to, and are inclined to see their main or sole task as the cultivation of Canadian political gardens, where there is obviously a lot that can be done without waiting for a rounded horticultural science. But this just pushes the question back one stage. Why is political science everywhere so immature? Why is there no body of received theory to which one can relate?

Many answers are possible. Some would put it down to the shallowness of the behavioural revolution and the affinity of behaviouralism to the materialist, maximizing, individualist culture of at least the leading North Atlantic country, the sheer size and wealth of whose political science establishment has given it a protected market and an overwhelming penetrative power. Others would attribute it to the intransigence of the traditional political theorists who could not be brought to terms with the tough vulgarity of the swarm of empirical work. Still others, looking at the evident failure of political science to contribute anything worthwhile to the solution of increasingly desperate political problems — Vietnam, urban blight, race conflict, ecological destruction, and the rest — would attribute both the lack of a general theory and the failure in practice to the unconcerned willingness of members of the political science establishment to sell themselves to the highest bidder — in the wealthiest countries often the government itself, whose need to cover up its failures to deal with these problems is likely to be greater, by the time the political scientists are enlisted, than its desire to do anything serious about them.

Among them, these answers to the question of why there is no accepted body of general theory in political science perhaps contain a sufficient explanation. The root of the explanation would be the aggressive, bourgeois individualist culture, which has been at its strongest in North America, especially in the United States, during the whole period when the tone of current political science was set, and of which it would be beyond the scope of this paper to offer in turn a further explanation.

Such a society neither demands nor welcomes serious discussions of the extent to which the going political system serves defensible social purposes and values. Nor does it want fundamental explications of the way its governing mechanisms actually work as functioning parts of the whole society. The first activity might call too much into question; the second might reveal too much. Such a society does not want the political system to be *understood*. It is, however, happy to have the system's superficial performance *measured*: that can be flattering, is technologically smart, and draws off much of the abundant energy of the political science profession. The political establishment can easily see to it that these preferences of the society are met.

All this may be deduced from the nature of the society, and observed in its behaviour. But can we find any particular factor more specific than this, through which the culture can be seen to have had this effect? I think we can, and fortunately it is something that is remediable by the profession itself, or will be if the profession's growing self-consciousness and its prospective increasing sense of the social responsibility of the intellectual make it receptive to this diagnosis.

The force I have in mind has operated in both the United States and Canada, somewhat earlier in the United States, then carried over into Canada. The process may easily be seen as the Americanization of Canadian political science, but that is a superficial view. It is not an Americanization but, in the pejorative sense, the modernization of political science by forces operating in both countries. I shall confine my remarks largely to the working of this factor in Canadian political science, as I have neither the space nor the competence to discuss the American phenomenon with any pretence to adequacy. I shall make some references to the American phenomenon, without intending to imply that the development of American political science, and its penetrative power, constitute a sufficient explanation of the Canadian development.

The process to which I refer may be described either as the abandonment of the political economy tradition or the lust for professional independence and discipline autonomy, especially independence from economics. The working of this factor in the Canadian profession is evident as soon as one looks back at the Canadian development of the last few decades with this hypothesis in mind. During the period of the quantitative flowering of Canadian political science this factor has plainly, if not always consciously, been strongly at work. The figures of the numerical growth of the profession cited earlier[26] suggest that there have been two main stages of growth since an indigenous Canadian political science was born; this birth I place in the 1920s and early 1930s.[27] Setting aside the minimal growth in numbers from 1930 to 1950, we can see two later stages of growth, slow in the 1950s, rapid in the 1960s (and increasingly rapid in the latter half of the 1960s).

As several of the published surveys of the development of Canadian political science have noted, a political economy tradition prevailed up to and through the 1930s. The high point was the Rowell-Sirois Commission, which dominated Canadian political inquiry in the latter part of the 1930s.[28] Its two academic members were first-generation Canadian political scientists, Henry Angus and R.A. MacKay, both of whom assumed that a realistic political science had to be at the same time political economy. The realism of that assumption about Canadian politics has been succinctly stated by Professor Smiley:

Public problems which agitated and continue to agitate Canadians – problems of external trade and natural resource development, of immigration and transportation and fiscal policy and so on – almost invariably presented themselves with both political and economic aspects, and if we add the complications of a division of powers between federal and provincial governments, usually a legal-constitutional dimension as well. Thus Canadian scholars discovered early what has become the necessary working assumption of those now studying the developing nations, i.e., that the disciplinary boundaries between economics, politics, and sociology could be maintained only in those geographical areas where there existed a relatively high degree of sub-system autonomy in respect to economy, polity, and society.[29]

The political economy tradition in Canadian political science began its sharp decline in the 1940s. One might be inclined to attribute the change to the influence of one outstanding Canadian scholar and teacher, Robert MacGregor Dawson, for there is no doubt that his own work and his influence on a whole generation of Canadian scholars was enormously effective.[30] He was not interested in political economy: one of his most admiring students, now a senior member of the Canadian political science establishment, described his interest as the nuts and bolts of the Canadian political system. I do not think MacGregor Dawson would have repudiated that description. His influence can be seen in the volumes of the first decade of the *Canadian Government Series*, which was launched in 1947 and of which he continued to be the editor until his death in 1958.

To suggest that the influence of one man changed the whole course of Canadian political science would be fatuous. Dawson was, I think – and I came to know him well during his years at the University of Toronto (1936-58 – driven on by sheer exasperation that nobody was paying attention to the nuts and bolts. Diagrams of them were essential. He had found a real lack in Canadian political science, and he was able to persuade his students of it. The lack was visible, and was seen. But no pervasive relation between the operation of the political system and the economic realities was seen. Dawson's political science remained diagrammatic.

What I am suggesting is that the move away from the political economy tradition can be explained not by the influence of one man so much as by the backwardness of Canadian political science down to the 1940s; that is, the scantiness of work actually accomplished, and the realization then of how much straight descriptive work had to be done to get anything like a full picture of the Canadian political system. That work was so absorbing for at least the next decade that questions of the relation of the institutions described to the economy and society were largely neglected.

The same pattern was followed as the political scientists began to extend their reach beyond the formal institutions of government. The move away from the political economy approach spread to broader fronts in the 1950s. As each new field was moved into – fields already developed in more mature countries – there was simply too much to be done, and it could apparently be done adequately with the methods and assumptions by which it had been developed elsewhere. At any rate, it needed those methods and it did not need political economy. The 1950s saw a substantial amount of work on Canadian political parties and movements, and the beginnings of electoral studies. Some of the work on political parties and movements adhered to a political economy approach[31] but much of it did not. The electoral studies, having to be started from scratch in the late 1950s and the 1960s, had such a virgin resource of electoral records that they did not need a political economy approach.

Political science proliferated very rapidly in Canadian universities during the 1960s, with a consequent heavy recruitment of young political scientists, many of them from the United States.[32] This growth brought into play a further pressure that had been inherent but latent in the absorption of the profession in narrowly political phenomena. The new thrust was a mounting desire for an independent status for political science, which meant independence from the economists.

One result was the splitting, in 1967, of the one association and one journal, each of which had served economists and political scientists together until then, into two associations and two journals. Underlying the separation (and used to justify it) was something more serious, namely, the assumption, taken over from the Americans, that political science was a science in its own right by virtue of having a distinctive subject-matter.

Much ingenuity has been used by American political scientists, in the last twenty or thirty years particularly, in staking out a territory distinct from any other social science. The behaviouralists and systems analysts felt that they had to establish their claims to a 'new' political science. The way to escape from the confines of studying *institutions* was to see politics as an *activity*. So something had to be found that would distinguish *political* activity from other kinds. Not wishing to work with 'the state' as the central concept, as the older political science had done, a formulation which had at least allowed some interest in the relation between the state and economic life, the new men in effect built walls between the study of the state and the study of the economy. One can see this in Easton's reference to 'a long line of writers who see that the characteristic of political activity, the property that distinguishes the political from the economic or other aspect of a situation, is the attempt to control others.'[33] The assumption that economic activities are not attempts to control others indicates both the unreality of this political science and the unlikelihood of its ever reconnecting the two activities it has so insistently put asunder.

The political scientists in question are not, of course, entirely to be blamed for making that assumption about economic activities, since that is the impression of economic life they might well get from current economic theory. By the same token, the political scientists are not entirely to be blamed for the separation of political and economic theory. The separation may have been inevitable because both disciplines had in their different ways become unrealistic; but if we persist in the separation we shall keep them both weak. It seems to me probable that they have both become unrealistic because that is what the society that is the market for their services has required.

It is now apparent that my argument has come full circle, from the point at which I asked why political science (generally, not just in Canada) is so immature as to have no body of received theory. I began with the question why political science, unlike economics, has no such body of theory. I mentioned some possible explanations, and suggested that they all came down to one: that the possessive individualist society neither demands nor welcomes fundamental understading of its political life. I then sought for a more specific factor in the Canadian practice of political science, and found it in the abandonment of the political economy tradition. That in turn was traced to (a) the realization, by Canadian political scientists in the 1940s, of the scantiness of Canadian empirical work, and the consequent need for a massive amount of straight political description; (b) the rapid recruitment of the Canadian profession in the 1960s, leading to an irresistable demand for professional independence from the economists; and (c) underlying that demand, the assumption, already dominant in the more advanced American profession, that political science has and must insist on having a unique subject matter which is not just 'the state', an assumption which led them to drain out of political science any political economy content or approach. And this, I have ended by suggesting, is what the society they are working in requires. So we are back at the possessive individualism of contemporary society as the fundamental explanation of the lack of a general theory in North Atlantic political science.

It may seem that I have explained too much, for I began with the contrast between the absence of a general theory in political science and the presence of one in economics, but have now said that the North Atlantic society requires unreality in both disciplines. Why, then, did not economics equally fail to produce a received general theory? The answer I think is that economics had already produced, in neo-classical economic theory, a body of theory which had so effectively shut out any social dimension of economic life that it easily met the requirement of unreality.

We are confronted, finally, with the question: what are the prospects for a more realistic political science, or, if you like, for a reintroduction to it of political economy? The present situation is lamentable because the present political science is incapable either of criticizing the society or of understanding it well enough to offer solutions to its most pressing problems.

There *is* now a prospect of change. For conditions within the most advanced of our capitalist democracies have become so revolting, and so clearly beyond the capacity of the old 'new' political science to solve, that a revolt within the profession is now on its way. One might cite the remarkable growth in the strength of the reform caucus in the American

Political Science Association, which last year fell short by only a handful of votes of winning the presidency of the Association. At least as remarkable is the change of heart in leading proponents of the behavioural revolution of the 1950s. I call Easton as my witness again. In his presidential address to the American Political Science Association in 1969, and in a following piece entitled 'Continuities in Political Analysis: Behavioralism and Post-Behavioralism',[34] he urged that the condition of American society required a new responsibility in political scientists, a responsibility which meant giving up (a) the pretence that political science is value-free; (b) the posture of pure scientists, aloof from policy issues (a posture which had always been false, in view of their willingness to sell their services to governments without questioning the uses to which their expertise would be put); and, less clearly, (c) the insistence that political science, to be pure, must be separate. Arguing that all these positions were rendered untenable by the social realities of the 1960s, Easton observes:

There can be little doubt that political science as an enterprise has failed to anticipate the crises that are upon us ... In some considerable measure we have also worn collective blinders that have prevented us from recognizing other major problems facing our discipline. For example, how can we account for the failure of the current pluralist interpretations of democracy to identify, understand, and anticipate the kinds of domestic needs and wants that began to express themselves as political demands during the 1960s? How can we account for our neglect of the way in which the distribution of power within the system prevents measures from being taken in sufficient degree and time to escape the resort to violence in the expression of demands ...? How can we account for the difficulty that political science as a discipline has in avoiding a commitment to the basic assumptions of national policy, both at home and abroad, so that in the end, collectively we have appeared more as apologists of succeeding governmental interpretations of American interests than as objective analysts of national policy and its consequences?...

There is no single explanation for the narrow vision of our discipline. We can, however, at least go so far as to offer this hypothesis: Whatever the reasons, the failure to broaden the vision of our basic research may

be due in good part to a continuing hesitation to question our normative premises and to examine the extent to which these premises determine the selection of problems and their ultimate interpretations.[35]

Later, he urges that

the need to escape the research limits imposed by the unwitting adoption of prevailing moral-political premises is more urgent than ever
before ... today knowledge brings with it new responsibilities; it leads to
a changing image of the role of the professional political scientist. [Not
only must he] seek to leave his impact on specific social policies, such
as racial tension, pollution, war, or hunger. His activities will be
responsible only if they are linked to broader conceptions of the kinds
of political systems that could be, systems in which such policies would
be more likely to be accepted or with which they could be consistent.[36]

Such a measured reappraisal of the responsibility of the political
scientists, coming from so influential a spokesman, is surely encourag-
ing. His manifesto does not specifically make the case that political
science should amend its unconcern with the economic life of a society,
although there is a recognition that 'political science alone is unable to
propose solutions to social problems; these normally involve matters
that call upon the specialized knowledge and skills of other social
scientists'.[37] But at least this kind of thinking opens the way to some
realistic reconnection of the study of political and economic life, which
had been blocked by the thinking of the last two or three decades.

I would even venture the prediction that any reformation along
these lines will come earlier in political science than in economics,
simply because political science cannot, whereas economics can, fall
back on the solace of a general theory which, however shortsighted and
culture-bound, has both theoretical elegance and considerable usefulness, to governments (which continually have to regulate the economic
mechanism) and to businesses (which can sometimes profit from employing it).

If the reformation comes to Canada, and the expectation is that it
will, it will be coming at a time when we are able to profit from it, as
we could not from the previous 'behavioural revolution'. For it will be

coming at a time when the Canadian backlog of empirical detail work, in such fields as political parties and electoral behaviour, has been substantially reduced. That is to say, we shall not be under the pressure which has, by my account, ever since the 1940s kept most Canadian political scientists from seeing the wood for the trees, and even from looking for the wood. So it should be possible for our empirical work to be done more consciously with a view to contributing to a general theory of at least the Canadian political system.

And since the reformation calls into question the adequacy of the pluralist model of society and the brokerage model of the political system, both of which have been so taken for granted by us[38] that many who use them do not realize that they are using them, we may break through what is now the main barrier to a realistic political science. We have only to recognize that they are value-laden models.

It is not that these models are entirely wrong. They do fit quite well any society – like the American and Canadian up till now – which is affluent, market-oriented, materially individualist, and careless of the consequences. But when, as now, these models are accepted and taught as self-evidently valid, they become justifications of that society and system. So they inhibit critical thought about the society, and leave us unprepared to cope intellectually, at any level of abstraction or application, with changes in it. Yet our societies are changing. They are becoming, or parts of them are becoming, more heedful of consequnces. If only parts of them do so, the society will move from pluralist to polarized. We should not assume that Canada is immune to polarization. We should rather anticipate it, and be prepared.

Although the foregoing might be construed as a plea for more interdisciplinary studies, it is not. For interdisciplinary studies are apt to be artificial and contrived, and are necessarily so when they start, as they now do start, from a base of jealous independence. It is rather a plea for the willing interpenetration of the disciplines of politics and economics, a plea for the renewal, on what could now be a higher plane, of the tradition of political economy.

APPENDIX: PROFESSIONAL INTERESTS

00 FOREIGN AND CROSS-NATIONAL POLITICAL INSTITUTIONS AND BEHAVIOR
01 Analysis of particular political systems or subsystems
02 Decision-making processes
03 Elites and their oppositions
04 Mass participation and communications
05 Parties, mass movements, secondary associations
06 Political development and modernization
07 Politics of planning
08 Values, ideologies, belief systems, political culture
09 Other

10 INTERNATIONAL LAW, ORGANIZATION AND POLITICS
11 International law
12 International organization and administration
13 International politics
19 Other

20,30 METHODOLOGY
21 Computer techniques
22 Content analysis
23 Epistemology and philosophy of science
24 Experimental design
25 Field data collection
26 Measurement and index construction
27 Model building
28 Statistical analysis
31 Survey design and analysis
39 Other

40 POLITICAL STABILITY, INSTABILITY, AND CHANGE
41 Cultural modification and diffusion
42 Personality and motivation
43 Political leadership and recruitment
44 Political socialization
45 Revolution and violence
46 Social and economic stratification
49 Other

50 POLITICAL THEORY
  51 Empirical theory
  52 Formal theory including game theory
  53 History of theory
  54 Normative theory
  59 Other

60 PUBLIC POLICY: FORMATION AND IMPACTS
  61 Domestic
  62 Foreign
  63 Military and national security
  69 Other

70 PUBLIC ADMINISTRATION
  71 Bureaucracy
  72 Comparative administration
  73 Organization and management analysis
  74 Organization theory and behaviour
  75 Personnel administration
  76 Planning, programming, budgeting
  77 Politics and administration
  78 Systems analysis
  79 Other

80,90 CANADIAN INSTITUTIONS, PROCESSES AND BEHAVIOUR
  81 Courts and judicial behaviour
  82 Elections and electoral behaviour
  83 Executives
  84 Interest groups
  85 Intergovernmental relations
  86 Legislatures
  87 Political and constitutional history
  88 Political parties
  91 Public law
  92 Public opinion
  93 Federal government
  94 Provincial government
  95 Municipal or regional government
  97 Other
  99 Political science

74 C.B. Macpherson

NOTES

1 Edmund Burke, *Reflections on the Revolution in France, Select Works*, vol. II
   E.J. Payne, ed. (Oxford, 1898), p.107.
2 *Transactions of the Royal Society of Canada, 1889* section 2, pp.3ff.
3 C.B. Macpherson, 'On the Study of Politics in Canada,' *Essays in Political
   Economy in Honour of E.J. Urwick*, H.A. Innis, ed. (Toronto, 1938),
   pp.147-65
4 C.B. Macpherson, 'The Position of Political Science,' *Culture*, III (1942),
   pp.452-9
5 R. MacGregor Dawson, *Report to the Social Science Research Council of
   Canada, October 1950*, now published in *CPSA Newsletter*, II (March 1973),
   pp.1-6; F. Watkins and B.S. Keirstead, *Report for UNESCO*, published in *Contemporary Political Science* (Paris: UNESCO, 1950), pp. 171-7; C.B. Macpherson, *Report for the International Political Science Association, June 1951*,
   published as 'L'Enseignement de la science politique au Canada,' *Revue française de science politique*, IV (1954), pp. 384-400. These three were reviewed
   by J.E. Hodgetts in *Canadian Journal of Economics and Political Science*,
   XVIII (1952), pp.88-92
6 C.B. Macpherson, 'The Social Sciences,' *The Culture of Contemporary Canada*,
   Julian Park, ed. (Cornell, 1957), 181-221
7 D.V. Smiley, 'Contributions to Canadian Political Science Since the Second
   World War,' *Canadian Journal of Economics and Political Science*, XXXIII
   (1967), pp.569-80; and J.E. Hodgetts, 'Canadian Political Science: A Hybrid
   with a Future?', *Scholarship in Canada 1967*, R.H. Hubbard, ed. (Toronto,
   1968), (this paper was given at the 1967 meeting of the Royal Society of
   Canada)
8 notably Christian Bay, whose paper 'Politics and Pseudopolitics: A Critical
   Evaluation of Some Behavioral Literature,' *American Political Science Review*,
   LIX (March 1965), pp.39-51, is a landmark
9 Smiley, p.571
10 F.F. Schindeler, *Responsible Government in Ontario* (Toronto, 1969)
11 An article by Professor Hull, based on this material appears in the March 1973
   issue of the *Canadian Journal of Political Science:* I am greatly indebted to
   him for making the material available to me in advance
12 C.B. Macpherson, 'L'Enseignement de la science politique au Canada,' *Revue
   française de science politique*, p.390
13 R.R. March and R.J. Jackson, 'Aspects of the State of Political Science in
   Canada,' *Midwest Journal of Political Science*, XI (November 1967), pp.434,
   435
14 J.E. Hodgetts, p.100
15 W.H.N. Hull, 'The 1971 Survey of the Profession,' *Canadian Journal of Political Science*, VI (March 1973), pp.89-120
16 Information supplied by CPSA

17 In political philosophy, twenty-one in progress 1971-2, twenty completed 1919-70; in parties and elections, twelve in progress 1971-2, eleven completed 1919-70

18 The classificatory scheme is reproduced as Appendix I.

19 The classification was in fact adapted from one made by the American Political Science Association, which was making a survey of the American profession at about the same time: the decision to use the APSA scheme was made with a view to comparability of the results of the two surveys. The significant fact is not the American origin but the Canadian response: sixty-two of the sixty-four subheads were used by respondent members of the Canadian profession.

20 Hugh Stretton, *The Political Sciences* (Routledge and Kegan Paul, 1969), p.65

21 One need only mention the work of F.M. Barnard, Christian Bay, Gérard Bergeron, Allan Bloom, David Braybrooke, Léon Dion, J.A.W. Gunn, C.B. Macpherson, Charles Taylor, and André Vachet.

22 Subsequently published in *Canadian Journal of Economics,* 1 (1968), pp.129-46

23 Thus while there are several references to Macpherson's book on a Canadian subject, there is no reference to his books on non-Canadian subjects, although the latter are more widely known and used (even in Canada) than the former.

24 Smiley, p.580

25 David Easton, *The Political System, an Inquiry into the State of Political Science*, second ed. (Alfred A. Knopf, 1971), pp.369-70

26 See above, p.72. The growth curve could be plotted more precisely by a close analysis of university calendars over the decades, but for our purposes the rough indications given by the figures cited will serve.

27 Cf. my contribution to Julian Park, ed., *The Culture of Contemporary Canada* (Cornell, 1957)

28 *Royal Commission on Dominion-Provincial Relations, Report* (Queen's Printer, 1940)

29 D.V. Smiley, p.569. Cf. my contribution to *The Culture of Contemporary Canada*

30 See J.H. Aitchison, ed., *The Political Process in Canada, Essays in Honour of R. MacGregor Dawson* (Toronto, 1963), for an indication of the extent of his influence

31 notably Macpherson's *Democracy in Alberta* (Toronto, 1953), which in the opinion of some critics at the time overdid it

32 The effect they produced was not due so much to their being Americans as to their being young (and numerous).

33 Easton, p.115. Cf. the comment on this in my *Democratic Theory: Essays in Retrieval* (Oxford, 1973), pp.46-7

34 both published as an Epilogue to the second edition (1971) of his *The Political System* (see footnote 25)

35 Easton, pp.338-9 (this is from the presidential address)

36 Easton, p.362 (this is from the 1971 essay)
37 Easton, p.336
38 With a few notable exceptions, e.g., Gad Horowitz, 'Conservatism, Liberalism and Socialism in Canada: An Interpretation, '*Canadian Journal of Economics and Political Science,* XXXII (1966), 144-71; and John Wilson, 'Politics and Social Class in Canada: The Case of Waterloo South,' *Canadian Journal of Political Science,* I (1968), 288-309

Commentary Y.F. ZOLTVANY

Let me begin by stating that I am not a political scientist but a historian. As such, I felt that it would be somewhat presumptuous of me to attempt to draw out the implications of Professor Macpherson's paper for political science. This can best be left to the members of that discipline who are present here today. What I did, this being the era of interdisciplinary studies and model building, was apply Professor Macpherson's explanation of the current state of political science to my own area of studies—French-Canadian history—to see what the results would be. This turned out to be an interesting experiment.

I chose to retain the following three points from the paper we have just heard:

1/ Political science today, as a body of knowledge, is immature and even unrealistic.

2/ The root cause is the aggressive, bourgeois, individualist culture which has been at its strongest in North America, especially in the USA, during the period when the tone of current political science was set. Such a society does not welcome a discussion of its value system.

3/ There is presently a prospect of improvement, because conditions within the most advanced of our capitalist democracies have become so revolting and so clearly beyond the capacity of old political science to solve. Likely to hasten the improvement would be a renewed osmosis between the discipline of politics and economics.

No one will dispute that the same could be said of the way French-Canadian history was written down to the 1950s. Indeed,

French-Canadian history well into that decade was the very quintessence of immaturity and unrealism. Professor Macpherson reminded us that he is not generally accounted an admirer of E. Burke. Well, I have some reservations about P.E. Trudeau, but I can only concur with a statement he made in *La Grève de L'Amiante*, 'In Quebec, during the first half of the twentieth century, our social thinking was so idealistic, so *à priori*, so far removed from reality and to be blunt, so ineffectual that it practically never became a real part of the community's living and evolving institutions.' French-Canadian historians painted an idealized picture of past society as virtuous, ruled by the Church, and rooted in the soil.

The basic cause of this state of mind was certainly not the prevalence of an aggressive, bourgeois, individualist culture. The French-Canadian elite rejected emphatically the bourgeois acquisitive ethos. 'Our mission,' wrote Mgr Paquet around 1900 in a text which has become famous, 'is less to handle capital than to stimulate ideas; less to light the furnaces of factories than to maintain and spread the glowing fires of religion and thought and to help them cast their light into the distance.' Statements like this one are legion.

A basic cause of this type of thinking was that the elite of French Canada were clerical and rural. They had to maintain alive the cult of values to which they owed their primacy. It seems that it is not only the bourgeois-liberal elite who do not welcome discussions of their value system.

But there may have been another, yet more fundamental reason for the behaviour of French-Canadian thinkers. Their society constituted a cultural minority. Their prime responsibility, as they saw it, was to strengthen it vis-à-vis the alien majority. That is perhaps why socialism, class struggle, etc. were dirty words in their vocabulary. Besides connoting godlessness and materialism they also connoted social divisions and that, above all else, was what French Canada could not afford. Thus, leftist intellectual currents which could have rejuvenated social analysis in Quebec were swept aside in favour of rightist ideologies, like the cult of the leader and corporatism, which would maintain unity, the condition of survival.

Inexorably, however, the urban-industrial revolution which began on a large scale after the first great war was eroding the traditional order and generating new class structures and new social and economic aspirations. In the 1950s French Canada belatedly entered the bourgeois-liberal phase of social development. The social sciences were transformed as a result. The writings of men like Guy Frégault and Fernand Ouellet in history, of Jean-Charles Falardeau in political science had a fresh, almost revolutionary quality to them. After all, there were so many false gods to attack, ancient myths to destroy. The periodical *Cité Libre*, which best exemplifies the spirit of the 1950s, trumpeted the manifest of this new generation of scholars.

> Liberate man from collective constraints
> Liberate the citizen from retrograde arbitrary governments
> Liberate consciences from an obscurantist church
> Liberate workers from capitalistic exploitation
> Liberate men crushed by authoritarian and obsolete traditions
> The revolution in Quebec will consist in the victory of personal liberties as inalienable rights, against capital, against the nation, against tradition, against the church, against the state.

During the 1950s and early 1960s the social sciences in Quebec were playing the role which must be theirs anywhere – they were explaining social processes. But that heroic age is dead. This brings me to point 3 of Professor Macpherson's paper. 'Will they now be happy,' to quote his words, 'to have the system's superficial performance measured?' I think not, for two reasons. First, liberal democracy was a latecomer to the French-Canadian scene and its roots in the soil of Quebec remain fragile. Many, especially in English Canada, deplore this but I personally see one major advantage in such a situation. It has left Quebec more receptive to other ideologies which have outflanked liberal democracy on the left. Secondly, for obvious linguistic and cultural reasons, French universities in Quebec have avoided massive Americanization. Their main source of inspiration in the field of social analysis – and this was enormously facilitated by cultural exchange programs launched during the Quiet Revolution – is coming from France. And in few countries have social considerations so penetrated the field of history. Discriminatory use of models drawn from French historical writing is one of the ways in which Canadian historical writing, both French and English, can remain, or become, realistic.

Commentary H.G. JOHNSON

The concept of a theory employed in Macpherson's paper is obviously in sharp contrast to that employed in my own and in economics generally. To the economist, a theory involves a proposition derived logically from assumptions, and is acceptable or not according to whether the facts of observation confirm it or disconfirm it. To Macpherson, on the other hand, a social science theory about a capitalist system – other than his own theory presumably – is either impossible because the system will not allow it to be formulated or possible only because it is completely irrelevant (contemporary political science exemplifying the one case and contemporary economics the other). This is a very comfortable position for the self-proclaimed political theorist to be able to take: social theories need neither be understood nor taken as a starting point for better theory construction, but may merely be dismissed with cleverly worded scorn; and the truth of the theory expounded is confirmed by the facts as the theorist alleges them to be or by the interpretation the theory requires him to put on commonly accepted facts, the crucial assertion in Macpherson's case being that in contrast to the pluralistic view of politics broadly assumed by the majority of his political science colleagues the polarization of political society postulated in his theory to be logically inevitable is on its way and they must get used to it. This, of course, is the methodology of evangelical religion and not of social science.

My assignment as a commentator on Macpherson's paper is to discuss the lessons to be taken from it for economics and other social sciences. I believe there are some lessons to be learned, at least in the form of cautionary historical experience, but the conclusions to be drawn from that experience are not those that Macpherson draws.

In my own paper, I emphasize the influence on the formation of contemporary economics of the discovery by governments in the English-speaking countries during the World War II of the usefulness of economics in the successful prosecution of an 'all-out' war by maximum mobilization of resources. In the United States, and to a rather lesser extent in the United Kingdom, this discovery of strategic usefulness to the state extended to the other social sciences as well. Anthropologists, for example, were pressed into service to advise on how best to motivate remote Pacific-island primitive tribal cultures to provide labour to service the American Navy and Air Force. And the social scientists responded willingly, as they accepted the objectives of the war effort in terms of national survival and victory. At the same time, they began to acquire the taste for the scientific professional status to which Macpherson refers. (It may be mentioned in passing that economists also acquired this taste and that a sense of inferiority in comparison with physical scientists led them for a time to sprinkle their professional debates and methodological discussions with jargon and concepts drawn from the natural sciences, as they understood them; but since they already possessed a fairly solid corpus of theory, demonstrably useful, they gradually found the effort to acquire status by imitating the language of the natural sciences unnecessary.)

Participation in a major war has been followed in the United States, in the cases of both World Wars, by a period of closure of national ranks and pressure for conformity with the American belief in the superiority of the American way of life, a belief closely associated with confidence in the power of American reliance on and willingness and ability to apply scientific methods. Emphasis on the scientific foundation of and use of scientific methods by American social science thus presented an obvious way of demonstrating the respectability in American terms of social enquiries that otherwise might be considered highly suspect. It also rationalized the provision of their services by social scientists to government and private enterprises. Economics and political science were, however, in vastly different positions with respect to their capacity to adjust to and take advantage of the necessary new emphasis on scientific method. On the one hand, as explained in my paper, economics was already primed for and moving towards the application of quantitative methods to the measurement and testing of significant relationships derived from a well-worked-out theory. Political science, by contrast, was not yet – and apparently has still not succeeded in becoming – armed with theories sufficiently clear and coherent to provide the foundations for non-trivial and important empirical research. Further, the fact that 'radical' economics neither lent itself nor attached importance to the formulation of empirically testable propositions about reality, made it easy to accept and even to be unaware of the submergence of radical economic ideas in the pressure for conformity. However, radical ideas were too strong and long-standing a part of the intellectual heritage of the subject to be completely ignored and forgotten; indeed, one can argue that the postwar concentration of economics on quantitative methods contributed greatly to the strengthening of the radical economics that has re-emerged in recent years.

On the other hand, economics had actually experienced the break-down of the economic system of capitalism in the form of the mass of unemployment and misery of the great depression of the 1930s; while this had apparently been met intellectually by the development of the Keynesian theory and its rapid and for the time being virtually complete conquest of academic economics, acceptance of the Keynesian revolution by the American political process still had to be won – and was not in fact won until the tax reduction of 1964. Consequently, the confidence of economists in the micro-economic allocative efficiency of the competitive capitalist system was subject to the important proviso that the possibility of macro-economic breakdown existed and could only be avoided by the pursuit of proper fiscal and monetary policies – which the political system fell far short of delivery. By contrast again, the American political and social systems had weathered the traumatic experience of the economic breakdown of the 1930s, and been validated by success in winning the World War II and by the ensuing dominance of the United States in the international political and economic system. Hence virtually unlimited confidence in both the superiority and the stability of the American democratic system ap-peared justified – and the confidence remained unbroken by repeated demonstrations of the inability of American political science to com-prehend and to forecast political developments in other countries, most notably the repeated breakdown of newly established political democ-racy in the 'new nations' into one or another form of one-party state.

Given this background of artificial assumptions, it is easy enough to understand both the quest of political science for a unifying theory, and its failure, and the reaction of despondency and self-questioning on the part of the profession to the disturbances that have occurred since the early 1960s in American political life – and also why the other social sciences have shared that reaction, with the notable exception of economics (despite the fact that the American Economic Association has experienced in common with other professional social science associations efforts by the radicals to take it over or at least to politicize it). In brief, economics has built into it an experience-based theory of what can go wrong with the American economic system, why it would happen, and how to remedy it, whereas political science has had no such experience and no such theory, and consequently became seriously disorganized when something did go seriously wrong with the American political system and American society generally.

Contrary to Macpherson's interpretation, however, what went wrong does not lend itself to interpretation in terms of his (traditional) concept of polarization of society and revulsion against its basic character strong enough to threaten revolution. Rather, at least as I would interpret it, there have been two strands in the recent development of dissatisfaction with the American way of life, neither of which really involves the foundations of potential revolution and both of which are – as experience has fairly rapidly shown – readily remediable by the traditional methods of democratic pluralism. One has been the realization by the groups directly concerned, and the communication of this realization to sympathetic and influential elements of public opinion through the methods of non-violent and violent protest, that certain groups in American society – successively the blacks, the poor and females – have been partially debarred from participation in the material benefits of American capitalism by discrimination against them of one form or another. Discrimination is no integral part of the system of competitive capitalism; instead it is a relic or residue of earlier more primitive forms of society. On the other hand, the conscious elimination of discrimination is no integral part of the system either, since its function is to promote the efficient fulfilment of people's desires by providing them with what they want to buy – though it does have a long-term effect by reducing discrimination precisely through 'depersonalizing' production and consumption through the replacement of direct personal relations between individual producers and consumers by the impersonal mechanism of the markets for products and for labour. If and when society becomes conscious of discrimination, averse to it, and anxious to eliminate it, the remedy is in principle a simple one: legislation, coupled with a willingness to bear whatever costs the effective elimination of discrimination may entail. Shortage of time precludes discussion of the economics involved and the pitfalls awaiting the adoption of naive legislative remedies. Suffice it to say that the outcome of concern about discrimination in the United States has not been revolution but legislation and accommodation to it by public opinion and social organization.

The other source of dissatisfaction with the American way of life has been the direct and indirect consequences of the war in Viet Nam; the direct consequences are the expression of the unwillingness of military-age, educationally accomplished males to risk the loss of the comfortable prospects of an assured privileged participation in the benefits of capitalism; the indirect consequences are a 'sour grapes' questioning of those benefits admixed with a self-interested desire to enjoy those benefits without the hard work and productive performance which the logic of the system exacts. Contrary to the frequent assertions of the radicals, war is no part of the inherent logic of capitalism, but a derogation from and denial of its prime function of increasing freedom by providing larger flows of want-satisfying goods and services; and the democratic solution to dissatisfaction with the unhappy consequences of war is to terminate the war, as has in fact happened. (Unfortunately, in the case of the war in Viet Nam, the motivations were a mixture of perceptions of national interests and perceptions of the need for some sort of world peacekeeping, and it may conceivably turn out that the American decision to withdraw from the war for domestic political reasons has been myopic and selfish from the point of view of preserving world peace – peace does not keep itself, any more than law and order results automatically from the nobility of natural man.) Similarly, concern for the environment and dislike of the rat race can be and are being implemented both by legislation and by the simpler devices of individual choice. The only problem is that those most concerned with the alleged evils are the most prone to assume that to remedy them is costless in terms of sacrifice of private consumption of goods and services, or that the sacrifice can be imposed on some other group to whom guilt can plausibly be attached.

In conclusion, I should not like my willingness to discuss Macpherson's contentions seriously to be taken to imply that I am naively unaware of what he is really up to, still less that I concur with his concept of scientific discussion – which is the antithesis of scientific. Like the Cambridge capital theorists referred to in my paper, he uses a facility with the language and concepts of his subject, and a certain minimal familiarity with what scientifically concerned scholars are doing, not to further the pursuit of truth, but to assert that his political position has a claim to truthfulness on a par with scientific truth. By taking his argument seriously, one concedes all that he wants, which is legitimation of his right to use the authority of his scholarly position to sell his political attitude and programme to the non-scholarly outside community. I must confess I find this charade distasteful, especially when circumstances compel me, as on this occasion, to play straight man to unscrupulous wit.

H.G. JOHNSON

3
The current and prospective state
of economics in Canada

The title of this paper was chosen in consultation with the Dean of
Social Science and various members of the Economics Department of
the University of Western Ontario to conform to the solemnity of the
opening of a new Social Science Centre at a university which has long
maintained a reputation for high quality of teaching and research in the
social sciences and whose Economics Department has become a serious
contender for the title of foremost in Canada. Unfortunately, however,
the title is unduly restrictive of the expression of the author's interests
in economics in Canada, resting as it does on the implicit assumption
that the geographical, ethnic, and cultural boundaries of the political
nation define a distinct national species of social science genus, suitable
for description, discussion, and evaluation. This probably is largely true
for such allied social sciences as political science, sociology, and anthropology, for which the existence and characteristics of the nation-state
define and indeed create a large part of the subject-matter of both
university teaching and scholarly research. (It is no accident that Canadian political scientists have traditionally been experts on federalism,
Canadian sociologists experts on French Canada and on minority group
cultures, and Canadian anthropologists experts on Eskimo and Cana-
dian-Indian cultures.) Indeed this used to be true of economics in the
golden age terminated by World War I, when literally a small handful of
economists in each of the European countries and imperial powers was
struggling to understand the characteristics and laws of operation of

industrial capitalism as it emerged in his own society, and to translate them into principles comprehensible to his fellow countrymen. But it is no longer true of contemporary economics — with the exception of a few ossified and highly politicized national professions typified by the French and the Italians.

In place of the great national 'schools' of economics of the past — typified by the English classical school, the Swedish school, the German historical school, the Austrian 'marginalist' school, the Italian school of public finance — contemporary economics can be classified, if one finds the exercise interesting, into three 'schools' corresponding broadly to three aggregates of nation-states. The first is scientific economics, the application of logic and quantitative methods to the understanding, interpretation, and prediction of economic phenomena. The second is Marxist economics, the entombment of a dead religious protest — a protest against the attribution of value in the form of an income share to material property whose owners incur no sweat as it renders its productive services — in the official ideology of a number of states with a strong tradition of arbitrary totalitarian government but otherwise bourgeois proclivities. The main tools of this school of economics are vituperation and emotive interpretation of historical and current events in terms of dogmatic stereotypes, along with, among the more scholarly inclined, the use of as much of the theory and methods of scientific economics as can be smuggled in past the ideological censors. The third school may be termed 'development economics' for brevity, though to do so is to ignore the work of many scientific economists and economic historians who have devoted themselves to the serious study of the sources of economic backwardness and the root causes of economic growth. It resembles very closely in many respects the pre-scientific mercantilist stage of the evolution of economic theory, most notably in its espousal of all sorts of governmental economic interventions as the only possible means of building an economically powerful nation-state. In modern times, however, belief in the miracle-working necessity of government intervention rests not so much on the fading remnants of belief in the divine right of kings to manage their national estates with a view to maximizing their capacity to overcome rivals, as on a mixture of several conditions: a tradition of benevolently paternalistic colonial government imposed on an authoritarian tribal structure; the replacement of imperial domination by political self-government without the necessary 'bourgeoisification' of the social and economic sub-structure; and an ideological super-structure taken over from both right-wing and left-wing critics of capitalism in the 1930s, who interpreted the politically inflicted collapse of the Great Depression as irrefutable evidence of the inherent self-contradiction of the capitalist system itself. The hallmark of this school of economics, apart from its abiding faith in the efficacy of government intervention unmitigated by the wealth of contrary evidence found in the experience of many countries, is its elevation of those carefully defined exceptions to general principles conscientiously recognized by serious scholars into general principles themselves, to which the scientific principles constitute negligible exceptions.

The purpose of this admittedly sketchy caricature is to make two serious points. The first is that, apart from a few amateurs self-appointed to the second oldest profession in the world and a vocal, sometimes near-lunatic fringe of competitively unviable academic scholars turned would-be cultural monopolists, economics in Canada is a local – and internationally reputable – representation of scientific economics as it has developed from its root origins in western Europe, especially the United Kingdom. The second is that, because of this fact, the title chosen for this paper suggests two alternative approaches, neither of which is really appropriate. One would consist of a lengthy catalogue of the kinds of research and publication Canadian economists have been involved in over the past decade or so, followed by a con-sidered statement of judgments concerning which areas have been neglected, which among those pursued deserve further effort, and which have been pursued past the relevant alternative-opportunity-cost point on the curve of diminishing returns. The objection to this ap-proach is that it implicitly assumes the desirability of scientific autarchy to the neglect of both economies of specialization and division of labour, and economies of scale. The other approach would involve comparing economics in Canada with economics in some other country, which would be objectionable as establishing that other country as a standard of excellence, and doubly objectionable because the country chosen as basis for comparison would obviously have to be the United States, and Canadians are adept at defining the ground rules so as to favour or disfavour Canadian efforts as required by the conclusion they want to draw.

The more appropriate approach, in my view, is to attempt to place the present and prospective state of economics in Canada in the broad perspective of the past and prospective evolution of economic science. To do so requires a general survey of that evolution, a recognition of special factors affecting how that evolution has manifested itself in Canadian professional life, and extensive reference to political influences and social-evolutionary forces which have shaped the character of the current practice of economics in Canada and are particularly important in discussing likely future developments. The relevant factors include not only certain tendencies or habits of thought in academic economics itself but political ideologies, the play of power politics between Europe and the United States and Canada's relation thereto, and the changing position of the university within society and in relation to government. Since these matters are admittedly not easy to weave together into a coherent pattern, this paper should be read as a suggestive essay rather than as a firmly scholarly study.

THE EVOLUTION OF ECONOMIC SCIENCE

A very brief sketch of the early stages of the emergence of economic science must suffice for present purposes.[1] The foundations of a scientific approach were laid by Adam Smith and the somewhat later English 'classical' economists, who – Ricardo in particular – shifted the emphasis from Smith's broad concern with the causes of the wealth of nations to the theory of distribution of the social product. Naturally enough, in view of the rather simple social structure of their time, they identified the income shares of factors of production with the income shares of social classes, namely landlords, workers, and capitalists. And while they had in some respects a clear understanding of the marginal principle of factor pricing, the principle was applied in Ricardian theory to the determination of the rent of land (the surplus of the average over the marginal product of labour applied to the land). Profits were treated as a second surplus equal to the excess of the marginal product of labour over the subsistence wage, the size of this surplus being determined by the stock of accumulated capital available to support labour at the subsistence wage. Such a theory implied that labour was being 'exploited' by being paid less than its product and it identified the productive contribution of the factor 'capital' with the income of a social class of capitalists. These assumptions and the resulting difficulties the classical economists had in separating interest ('profits' in their terminology) – the price needed to be paid for the use of resources in processes extending over time because the accumulated stock of such resources was scarce – from the ownership of such resources provided the starting point for Marxian theory and the many analytical confusions it has perpetuated. (It may be remarked in passing that the scarcity of the stock provides no ethical basis for the ownership of it, any more than does ethical objection to the ownership provide grounds for denying the scarcity of the stock itself, though either way around there are questions about the effects of remedial policies on incentives to accumulate and to use resources efficiently. The pseudo-problem is essentially an English creation: contemporary and later non-British writers have evinced a much clearer understanding of the economic nature of profits and interest.)

The so-called neo-classical successors of the English classical school, thanks to progress in understanding of the power of the differential and integral calculus among the educated, transformed the simple classical theory. A social-class-oriented schema based on specific theories for the supplies of the different (class-identified) factors of production was converted into a unified theory of the logic of choice, applying the principle of marginalism to consumer choice among commodities and producer choice among factors of production. Unfortunately the dominant English figure of the time, Alfred Marshall, chose to water down the underlying general equilibrium conception of his analysis into the partial equilibrium concepts of demand and supply in particular markets assumed to be too small for market interdependence to matter. Thus he hoped to make his analysis accessible to the ordinary business man thirsting for economic understanding. Moreover, Marshall disguised the truly revolutionary implications of his approach in destroying the classical economists' identification of factors of production with social classes – partly out of excess scholarly modesty (some might say inverted scholarly snobbery) and partly as a result of a new methodology derived from biology rather than Newtonian mechanics.[2] Nevertheless, in the hands of the Cambridge school, headed by Marshall and including such men as Sidgwick and Pigou, economics appeared to have reached something close to scientific completion before the outbreak of World War I, and consequently the agenda for future development consisted of the empirical research and the study of economic history recommended to his pupils by Marshall himself. An important contribution to the completion of the scientific structure was Pigou's economics of welfare,[3] which elaborated on a minor theme of Marshall's — 'externalities', or divergences between private and social costs or private and social benefits under the working of a competitive capitalist system — and built a substantial part of the analysis on the proposition, assumed to be derivable on strictly scientific grounds from the principles of utilitarian philosophy, that economic welfare was indisputably increased by a reduction in the inequality of distribution of income.

The 'Cambridge synthesis', if it may be so called, remained dominant for a considerable period after academic business as usual resumed after World War I. Yet the seeds of revolutionary new developments existed in the interstices of the synthesis and came to fruition as a result of the work of the new postwar generation of toilers in the vineyard, in a short period of intense intellectual ferment roughly spanning the 1930s.

The first of these striking new developments, the imperfect or monopolistic competition revolution,[4] grew out of the failure of Marshall and Pigou to reconcile the existence and behaviour of the individual industrial firm with the model of perfect competition. The solution was found, after much debate about the characteristics of firms' cost curves, in the positing of a downward-sloping demand curve for the individual firm, reflecting imperfect substitutability between the characteristics of the firm's products and those of other firms' products.[5] The new theory, incidentally, prompted increased use of geometry and of elementary calculus as integral parts of elementary economic theory, since the core of its analysis of imperfectly competitive firm equilibrium was the equation of marginal cost and marginal revenue. The English development of the theory by Joan Robinson was markedly different in tone, if not in central analysis, from the American development by Edward Chamberlin. The former stressed the adverse welfare implications of imperfect competition: 'exploitation' of other factors by the entrepreneur in the form of payment by marginal revenue product (below value of marginal physical product), the alleged allocative inefficiencies of differentiation of products produced at greater than minimum possible costs, and more generally, as the theory developed, the absence of a rationale other than 'monopoly power' for the payment of profits. The American version was more eclectic and, in my view, more sensible on these issues.

The second revolution was the welfare economics revolution. As already mentioned, Sidgwick and Pigou had treated the assumption that a more equal distribution of a given total income improves welfare as a proposition resting on the same solid scientific foundations as propositions in positive economics. In reality, it was merely an expression of the Christian tradition as mediated through the sensitive Victorian social conscience; and it was devastatingly challenged by Lionel Robbins,[6] who pointed out correctly that anything economists may say about the desirable distribution of income represents a value judgment with no scientific foundation. As usual, however, nature abhors a vacuum, and her minions in the shape of able young theorists rushed in to replace utilitarianism with apparently scientific 'compensation tests' designed to detach the question of the effects on economic distribution of changes wrought by government policy from scientific positive economic evaluation of such changes. The attempt proved unsuccessful, in a broad sense; but it clarified the nature of the basic problem and incidentally resurrected the concepts developed by Pigou for dealing with the theoretical ramifications of the simple observation that 'smoke is a nuisance.'

The third revolution may alternatively be described as the 'general equilibrium' or the 'mathematical economics' revolution, which was introduced into the English language tradition from the continental European tradition primarily by J.R. Hicks and R.G.D. Allen.[7] The dual description reflects the fact that, while Marshallian partial equilibrium analysis, even in its offshoot form of monopolistic competition theory, could be expounded with the aid of elementary applications of the Euclidian geometry to which most schoolboys were exposed, analysis of the complex interdependencies among the parts of the economic system requires explicit use of advanced algebra. Fortunately, the process of 'working down' initially difficult frontier analysis from the post-graduate research level through the undergraduate college curriculum back into the high schools has provided an increasing flow of students capable of working with general equilibrium theory and its requisite mathematical system.

The fourth revolution was the 'empirical economics' revolution, by all odds the most important in the long run in the shaping of contemporary economics. Economics, at least academic economics in England, originated as an offshoot of moral philosophy, and as such was concerned primarily with the establishment of correct principles and the validity of logical deductions. This concern was given a new life by the imperfect/monopolistic competition revolution, with its emphasis on the implications of theoretical assumptions, and survives in bastard form in the English tradition today in the continuing habit of denying a theorist's conclusions by questioning the realism of his assumptions. By the time of Marshall, as has been noted, the main outlines of theoretical economics appeared to have been blocked out – with the important exception of monetary theory, which was reasonably well developed but which Marshall never got around to synthesizing properly – and the next stage of development, as Marshall recommended, appeared to be empirical verification and measurement through careful sifting of contemporary facts and the study of economic history. Such tasks were in fact what Marshall's pupils initially set out to execute. But the techniques of statistical analysis, especially regression analysis, were in their infancy and in any case not readily accessible to economists initially trained in classics, philosophy, history, or literature. In addition, World War I left England with an acute shortage of the high-quality talent required for the task of empirical work on contemporary economic problems, and with enough pressing problems of economic policy to preoccupy the gifted with pure and applied theorizing, so that the Marshallian agenda came to concentrate on the study of economic history (some of which was undoubtedly brilliant) and the history of economic thought (much of which was not). The fulfilment of the Marshallian agenda as far as 'applied' or 'empirical' study of economics was concerned had to wait on the development of the statistical tools of econometrics, the emergence of a sufficiently large group of economists capable of using these tools, and expansion of the numbers of the profession to the point where highly able men would perforce have to make their professional reputations on the basis of empirical studies, or at least support their theoretical arguments with acceptable empirical evidence.

The fifth and most rapidly pervasive revolution was the Keynesian revolution.[8] In the hindsight perspective of history, the Keynesian revolution derived its success largely from the failure of English monetary theorists to apply the perfectly adequate monetary theory they had at their disposal, a failure stemming in part from that trust in the superior competence of 'the authorities' and belief in the moral obligation to support the government characteristic of British economists in the shell-shocked interwar period and of many of them even now, and from Keynes's propensity to develop a new theory whenever the old one proved unsalable. In addition, the governments in Britain and America failed to act on the sensible advice of disinterested professional economists and economists and others tended to backslide into microeconomic explanations of macro-economic developments. Thus the chronic British interwar depression and the chronic depression of the 1930s everywhere became attributed not to the mistaken overvaluation of the pound in the one case and the failure of federal reserve policy and consequent collapse of internatioal liquidity in the other, but to a fundamental defect of the capitalist system -- its inability to maintain an adequate level of employment — requiring a new theory of aggregate demand which laid heavy stress on the need for proper management of fiscal policy while minimizing (contrary to Keynes's own views) the potentialities of monetary policy. The Keynesian revolution provided the requisite theory and also grafted onto welfare economics a new and crude concept of economic welfare as consisting primarily of full employment of labour in its accustomed jobs. This was a direct reflection of the most apparent and remediable source of social misery in interwar Britain, and of the autocratic patrician belief of Keynes and his colleagues in the British elite that social happiness consisted of a well-ordered economic world in which the lower orders, if deserving, were entitled to jobs and incomes appropriate to their appointed places in the system. Full employment is an extremely crude definition of welfare from any point of view, disregarding as it does questions of the quality of life and equality of opportunity in employment, freedom to pursue better opportunities at the cost of temporary measured unemployment, alternative and more effective methods of securing economic justice through fiscal income redistribution and social security measures, and the socially costly inflationary effects of a government guarantee of a politically defined full employment target. Much of the contemporary confusion in policy debates over inflation versus unemployment stems from failure on the part of those concerned to recognize the crudity of 'full employment' as a social welfare index.

Viewed against the intellectually revolutionary background of the 1930s the development of economics since World War II can be seen broadly as a process of integration and consolidation of the results of the various revolutions that occurred then. This process has been based on a vast expansion of the numbers and deepening of the professional training of economists, against the background of a growing supply of students capable of absorbing the mathematical and econometric techniques required, which has owed much to the prior development of formal instruction to the PhD level in the leading universities of the United States and the receptiveness of these graduate departments to foreign students. It has also owed much to the pervasive influence of competition for professional status and acclaim in a profession expanding rapidly, in the latter decade and a half of the period, in terms of both numbers of people and numbers of institutions. These factors raised some of the important questions about prospects for the future, to be discussed below; for the present discussion, it is enough to record that the mathematical and empirical revolutions have won the day, in the sense of establishing some degree of mastery of the relevant sets of tools as essential to the practice of the profession. This remark needs to be qualified, however, in the sense that partial equilibrium theory rather than elementary general equilibrium theory continues to dominate elementary teaching and policy analysis and the analysis of key problems in certain specialized fields of economic analysis, notably public finance, industrial organization, and labour economics. One of the most confident predictions that can be made about the future development of economics is that eventually economic analysis will come to be taught, and research into theoretical and applied problems in particular specialized fields approached, in terms of a general equilibrium framework — one that includes money as a specific element in the framework rather than employs the traditional assumption that money serves only as a veil over an essentially barter equilibrium.

Of the three revolutions concerned with the content rather than the method of economics – the imperfect competition, the welfare economics, and the Keynesian – the monopolistic competition revolution has fared least well. Its main thrust was in any case at the level of welfare economics rather than positive economics – and even at that level it raises complex questions once it has been admitted that consumers may prefer more variety at the expense of higher production costs. Moreover, its main strength in this respect came from the use of the unexplored concept of 'product differentiation' by competing firms, a phenomenon which subsequent theory tends to view in terms not of monopoly power possessed by the producer, but of competitive efforts by individual producers to develop a product with a combination of characteristics most appealing to (informed) consumers' tastes. The main residue of that revolution lies at the level of what may be termed 'popular' or 'radical' welfare economics: on the one hand supporting the long-standing radical view that profits are an economically functionless category of income derived arbitrarily from 'monopoly power' (sources unspecified); on the other hand confirming the pseudo-radical but essentially conservative view that the mass of the public does not know what it wants and hence, in the absence of culturally superior tutelage, allows its wants to be created and manipulated by commercial advertising. In the realm of positive economics, the imperfect/monopolistic competition revolution has had virtually no lasting impact. Theory and research have returned to the classical problems of monopoly and duopoly or oligopoly – especially the latter, which dominates the modern as contrasted with the classical economic scene. Since it is easily shown that under static conditions a duopoly or oligopoly market structure will behave like a single monopolist, with qualifications introduced by legal restrictions on inter-firm transfers of profits, recent contemporary work in this field has been concerned with the effects of disturbances introduced by technical progress and the uncertainty surrounding it, and with the economics of the problems of acquiring or conveying information about consumer wants and available products and about the behaviour of firms.

The welfare economics revolution, as already mentioned, fizzled out early in the post-World-War-II period after a display of theoretical pyrotechnics in the development and critical discussion of various compensation tests, the results of which may be described rather unkindly in the dictum that one cannot say that welfare has improved unless it actually has improved.[9] Even in the most comprehensive possible compensation test, all one can say is that society could be better off if it chose – but it might be a lot worse off if it left things to nature; and a famous proposition due to Kenneth Arrow[10] is that society may be unable to choose, by any normal voting procedure. Nevertheless, economists have continued happily in practice to make welfare judgments anyway, on the empirical basis that if one cannot arrive at and impose one's own value judgments scientifically, one can always treat the value judgments of groups in society as objectively determinable and applicable. This process has been facilitated by the fact that, until very recently at least, there has been little fundamental political cleavage in western societies (or more narrowly Anglo-Saxon countries) over the broad outlines of the 'mixed' or 'welfare' state based on progressive income taxation and a social security system. Consequently differences in value judgments have played a marginal rather than a central role in public policy debates (as they must, in a functioning democracy).

At the formal theoretical level, concern with 'compensation tests' and 'potential welfare' has been succeeded by work pushing the frontiers of economics in more fruitful, less negative and sterile, directions. First, the Paretoan 'first-best' welfare conomics was concerned with conditions for a welfare maximum, and implied – though this was frequently not understood – that fulfilment of these conditions on a piecemeal basis would not necessarily lead to welfare improvement, a point crucial to most practical policy situations. The subsequently developed theory of 'second-best'[11] is concerned with precisely the nature of the policies required in particular subsectors of the economic system to move society towards a higher level of welfare when the application of 'first-best' policies in other related sectors is precluded. (Cases in point are the use of the tariff to compensate for an institutionally imposed wage differential between the subsistence-exporting and the manufacturing-import-competing sectors in a developing country, and the use of transfers in kind to relieve poverty when cash subsidies to the poor are opposed by public opinion.)

Second, it has come to be realized that a large number if not all of the 'externalities' on which Pigovian welfare economies and its modern successors concentrate derive from the arbitrary assumption both that property rights are so allocated that owners are not obliged to absorb or empowered to appropriate all the effects of their decisions and that this situation is unalterable. Contemporary theorists regard property rights as marketable or exchangeable, and as being supported by legal rights to damages, so that the general case for state intervention based on assumedly ubiquitous 'externalities' is reduced to specific cases involving ambiguous or undefined property rights or uneconomically high transaction or litigation costs.[12]

Third, the main tradition of welfare economics takes a Benthamite or Fabian view of the state as a dispassionate and all-wise modern equivalent of Plato's philosopher-king, correcting the errors of his subject society by appropriate taxes, subsidies, and lump-sum transfers of income. A recently emerging school of theorists,[13] however, has been absorbing political into economic theory by treating the franchise as a second system of property rights (in addition to rights in material property) and the public as exchanging votes for policies with the political parties seeking election and power. This frame of reference permits the use of much of the elementary apparatus of economic theory but places special emphasis on the costs involved in the acquisition, dissemination, and appraisal of information. Note the substantial difference between this concept of the state as a type of market process and the Marxist concept of the state as an instrument of the ruling class. In this area, as in the economic, Marxism has failed to update its concepts and relate them to the contemporary facts of social organization, in spite of its claim to being 'scientific.'

Finally, as the state has come directly and indirectly to control a growing share of the national income and to seek to serve multiple social objectives, applied welfare economics, considered the theoretical core of 'public finance', has become a subject of much enlarged social importance, and one to which traditional 'public finance', with its primary orientation towards the fiscal needs of the sovereign, has still to make the major part of the required adjustment. (It is no wonder that the discovery and recruitment of 'a good senior public finance man' bulks so large in the perspective planning of a number of Canadian economics departments; nor that, thanks to the Royal Commission on Taxation and previous economic commissions, Canada is probably better equipped with good though relatively junior public finance specialists and Canadian economics with a general understanding of the subject, than the United States.)

Turning finally to the Keynesian revolution in monetary economics, it too has been going through a process of synthesization, even though the publicity courted and received by Milton Friedman and more generally the 'monetarist counter-revolution' might lead the casual observer to consider the monetary field as a morass of unsettled questions in political economy.[14] In fact, both the more sophisticated Keynesians and the quantity theorists of contemporary times have absorbed Keynes's basic monetary-theoretic contribution: that money is a form of wealth, and that the demand for it is a manifestation of optimum portfolio choice, subject to the yields and uncertainties connected with various assets as alternative forms for holding wealth. Keynes's claim to have established the general likelihood of less-than-full-employment equilibrium, with the full employment 'assumed' by the 'classical' economists as a special case, has become a minor issue, largely semantic or methodological, from the scientific point of view. It is, moreover, an irrelevant side-issue from the point of view of economic policy, largely because the western world has maintained a close-to-full-employment, uncomfortably inflation-prone environment for over a quarter of a century – whether owing to the successful propagation of Keynesian analysis and policy proposals or owing to the natural resilience of capitalism in the absence of suicidal monetary mismanagement is an open question. The controversy that remains in the field is concerned not with fundamentals of scientific analysis but with the propensity of Keynesians, as a majority coalition (like the Canadian Liberal Party) united by felt sentiment rather than thought-out principle, to neglect the intricate monetary side of Keynes's *General Theory* and to concentrate on the simple and misleading income-expenditure side in making current policy recommendations. To the 'vulgar Keynesian' endorsement of full employment as a policy objective and fiscal policy as the means to achieve it, the quantity theorists naturally juxtapose the inflationary consequences of full employment and the powers for good or ill of monetary policy. There is, however, one aspect of the synthesis at the theoretical level that remains to be completed: that pertaining to the theory of the balance of payments and international adjustment. This will require that the Keynesian approach, which is essentially an income-expenditure approach based on 'elasticity' responses to real relative price changes induced by divergent price-level trends or exchange-rate adjustments, be reconciled with the traditional 'monetary' approach in terms of self-correcting international money flows and purchasing-power-parity.[15]

SOME POLITICAL AND IDEOLOGICAL INFLUENCES
ON CONTEMPORARY ECONOMICS

The development of any discipline concerned with man as a social animal is inevitably influenced by the evolution and characteristics of the contemporary milieu. Scholarship itself is a luxury good, in economic terminology, social support of and interest in which is, broadly speaking, an increasing function both of the level of average income and of the concentration of income distribution. Scholars themselves are part of their society and are influenced by their role in it. This has become an increasingly important influence as the evolution and secularization of post-industrial revolution society has transformed universities from isolated centres for the training of young men for the priesthood and the gentry and for storing in celibacy scholarly eccentrics oriented however vaguely towards eternity, into institutions involved in the training of an ever-growing industrial as well as clerical and governmental elite. Universities have themselves become the respected lodging of the intellectual elite, enjoying an increasing monopoly of cultural eminence as society has implemented the principle of specialization and division of labour. Thus history tends to be rewritten from generation to generation to reflect the prevailing mood (usually majority, sometimes minority) of the times, albeit rewritten according to rising professional standards in the use of historical evidence, while English literature, being a happy hunting ground for those interested in quaint manners and morals or in recognizably truthful human experience, has recently been re-examined for the intellectual benefit of the Women's Liberation Movement. Economics, as a combination of social science and moral

philosophy concerned with man's means of meeting his most fundamental requirement – physical survival, both personal and social – has
been particularly subject to feedback processes operating between
scholarship and society. This section attempts, in a rather impressionistic way, to state and discuss the more important of these influences of
society, broadly conceived, on economics. Some are more obvious than
others, but nevertheless in my judgment are important, especially for
what they suggest about the future. I divide the discussion into three
major categories: government and economics, government being viewed
as society's major agency of influence and used as shorthand for the
broader manifestations of public opinion; academic politics in economics; and ideological influences on economic controversy.

Government and economics
Government has played an important supporting role in the expansion
and professionalization of economics since World War II, in several
major respects.

First, during World War II, Keynesian economics triumphed over
conventional 'financial' approaches to war-time economic management
and governments became deeply involved in economic planning and
administration, including the widespread use of controls over wages,
prices, and allocations of materials and foreign exchange (at least in the
English-speaking countries). Such developments vastly increased the
respect for and use of economists in the government service. Perhaps it
would be fairer to say that in the name of and under the leadership in
Britain of Keynes himself, governments applied, at the aggregate level
of total available resources, the long-standing concern of economics
with the budget constraint on the allocation of scarce resources and its
understanding that money is merely a veil – sometimes deceptive and
mischievous – over the interaction of unlimited wants with limited
resources, since Keynesian methods of war-time monetary and financial
management planted and watered the seeds of postwar inflation. Moreover, the increased governmental demand for trained economists proved
permanent. In contrast to World War I, which followed a long period of
sustained prosperity and social self-content and hence appeared as a
temporary interruption followed by a return to business (including
government business) as usual, World War II was preceded by an

unusually deep and prolonged depression which shifted public opinion strongly towards supporting a continuing vastly enlarged role of government in the society and in the economy. Note in passing that, owing to the operation of Parkinson's Law, war or any other reason for the temporary expansion of government tends to leave a permanent residue of expanded government. But the expansion that followed World War II reflected not merely the inherent laws of bureaucracy but a major change in social attitudes. This change had two aspects: assignment to the government of responsibility for achieving the major macro-economic objectives of full employment, price stability, and economic growth (and on the Canadian list of objectives, greater equality of income distribution); and assignment to the government of operational responsibility for or planning and regulatory control over large sectors of the economy, on both the producing and consuming sides of economic activity (as examples, natural resource development on one side, health care and social insurance on the other). Both assignments, it may also be remarked, have tended to have a long-run disintegrative effect on countries with federal constitutions (Canada and the United States), in the form of efforts to shift economic powers towards provincial and state governments; and on countries with unitary constitutions, in the development of regional nationalism and the demand for devolution of powers. The primary reasons have been, on the one hand, the differential regional impact of macro-economic management policies and the desire to escape from or compensate for errors of central decision-taking by an appeal to lower and more politically sensitive levels of government; and on the other, the fact that as society waxes in affluence its social concerns become more localized and hence more the province of local than of central governments.

The role of government as the major employer of trained economists, especially those with one or more graduate degrees, exercises a variety of influences on the teaching and professional practice of academic economics. Progress and the maintenance of professional scholarly standards in a subject with the characteristics described in the previous section depends in a familiar way on economies of specialization and division of labour, which in turn depend on department scale; this includes the externalities which accrue from the regular (but not too proportionally large) recruitment of newly trained people to existing departments. The existence of a steady and substantial govern-ment demand for the product has both permitted the enjoyment of these economies, and provided a larger pool of talent from which to select the academic economists of the future, by affording a safe alter-native route to those who fail to make the academic grade to success. On the other hand, the presence of a large-scale government demand for the product cannot help but bias the tone or ethos of the subject towards conservatism, through notions among both students and faculty of the useful as contrasted with the 'airy-fairy' aspects of the subject. Radicalism tends to get hived off into peripheral optional sub-jects or safely shackled into the discipline of elementary bread-and-butter teaching – if it does not quit academic life entirely out of sheer boredom with prosaic minds applying technical steam-hammers to the cracking of intellectual nuts. (Of course, conservatism eventually be-comes the psychological bent of almost anyone who devotes his life to the study of how a system works.) The presence of an assured market for economists in government service, in contrast to the position con-fronting students in other social sciences, especially sociology, accounts, in my judgment, for the universally contrasting behaviour of students and faculties in economics and the other social sciences during the 'student troubles' of the late 1960s.

One particular aspect of the importance of government as a large-scale employer of economics graduates in Canada and the United King-dom, relevant especially to the present and prospective state of the subject, is worth noting at this point for later discussion. In both countries, government has come to respect the superior technical quali-fications and seriousness of purpose of the MA-holder or all-but-thesis-qualified PhD candidate over the BA-holder, and is accordingly more or less happy to support graduate work to the MA level. But it is not convinced of the training value of the writing of the dissertation itself, and even regards the PhD-holder as constituting an awkward item to digest into the civil service apparatus. This creates a conflict between the academic interest in lower-level graduate work, as preparation for the PhD and a research-oriented subsequent career, and the social interest in lower-level graduate work as reflected in the marketplace, a conflict which has serious implications for the planning of institutional develop-ment of economics in a period of increasing financial stringency for universities.

One reflection of this conflict is that the 'ABD" ('all-but-dissertation') standard of professional qualification tends to become the *de facto* standard both of graduate student aspiration and of academic appointment. This has created perennial problems for Canadian departments in universities such as Western Ontario and Queen's, which have been trying seriously to elevate themselves to first-rank international status by insisting on high standards of research performance by staff and graduate students, only to have many of both groups drain off to other Canadian universities content with ABD qualifications for staff appointment and tenure. In Britain the picture is even more extreme: possession of a PhD by those who make their careers in that country (in university or elsewhere) frequently denotes insufficient competence, personal charm, or quickness of wit, to achieve academic appointment without one (though often the PhD is necessary to enable the student from a backward country to break into the charmed concentric circles of British academic life).

In addition, the dominance of a fairly steadily growing governmental demand means that the total demand for ABDs and PhDs is geared by a species of accelerator mechanism to the rate of change of the demand for academic economists, and hence to the rate of change of (predominantly undergraduate) enrolment, thereby incorporating strong elements of the 'corn-hog' cycle into the process of expansion of graduate work and complicating the planning problems of both departments and university adminstrations.

A second way in which government has influenced the evolution of professional academic economics has been through the large-scale use it has made of economists to conduct research into a wide variety of policy problems. Here a sharp distinction must be made between the British practice and the North American. The British practice typically employs economists to research 'in-house' on policy problems regarded as too sensitive for the results to be made public (except occasionally for defensive purposes) and hence distracts good economists from regular academic research without yielding subsequent benefits to the advancement of the subject in the form of published research results. The North American practice, on the contrary, typically involves treatment of the economist as a hired professional expert with the right or even guarantee of subsequent publication. This procedure has in my judgment had a very beneficial effect on the whole in the development of the North American and particularly Canadian profession, in providing immediate incentives for research, a specific topic and a deadline for delivery, and sustained supervision by and contact with other professional researchers, none of which are provided at all adequately to graduate students, especially junior staff in either Canadian or most American graduate departments. On the other hand – a point made to me forcefully by Grant Reuber a decade or so ago – the dominance in Canada of government as a source of research money for economists, and the influence of this dominance on standards for the award of Canada Council and private research grants, tends to divert professional attention away from basic theoretical and/or 'curiosity-oriented' research, thus making the Canadian profession less independent and less interesting to economists in other countries than it could be.

This weakness is most evident in two respects: one is the tendency of Canadian theorists to become competent combat troops in intellectual wars whose strategy is planned in other countries, the danger of which I shall illustrate later; the other is the temptation to Canadian academics with either insufficient professional competence by present standards or a taste for easy popularity among the masses to take the ready route of imitating and regurgitating the unscholarly and rabble-rousing pseudo-intellectual outpourings of their opposite numbers in foreign countries, predominantly in the United States but also in the failed and bitterly jealous quondam rival empires of the United Kingdom and France. It would be extremely difficult to discern, from the shallow and frequently near-psychotic writings of some Canadians, employed in otherwise reputable economic departments, on such subjects as American investment in Canada and the destruction or pollution of the environment, that serious Canadian economics scholars have achieved world-wide professional recognition for their contributions to the economics of resource utilization and of the multinational corporation.

A third, and important, way in which government has exercised a controlling influence over the development of economics to its present professional status has been through providing financial support, direct or indirect, for graduate students in this and other subjects. Direct support means cash maintenance of students; indirect support refers to the provision of part-time or full-time positions in the teaching of undergraduates, research assistance, etc. These tend to expand or contract together. There have been two major waves of such support. The first, immediately after World War II, was associated with the public belief in the English-speaking countries that those who had served in their countries' armed forces were entitled to special opportunities, particularly educational opportunities, to re-establish themselves in civilian life. This contributed greatly to the emergent dominance of the British (now American) tradition in economics, in contrast to the various continental European traditions, which till fairly recently remained fettered by the medieval traditions and social formalism of the University. It also introduced into the University – at least in economics – a new type of personality, broader in social origins and experience, and pragmatic and professional rather than scholastic in its approach, one result being greatly to reduce the gulf created by the traditional university between the academic scholar and the man of affairs. (The longer-run effects of this transformation, reinforced by the next wave of government support, have since become a focal point of radical-student criticism: radical students, being an unselfconscious social elite, tend naturally to be appalled by the consequences of social democratization.)

This first wave of governmental support for scholarship, including academic economics, derived from an interpretation of democracy's obligations to its warrior-citizens, not from any perceived or actually realized need for a vast expansion of the proportion of the population qualified by higher degrees. It was succeeded by nearly a decade of lean years characterized by low real salaries and slow promotion for academics. During this period many drifted or were dislodged out of academic life into other pursuits, especially the civil service, where they constituted a hidden reservoir of senior talent available for employment in the next wave of expansion. Those who remained in academic life, whether through superior talent and devotion or through lack of alternatives as cosy as low-level academic tenure, eventually cashed in heavily on expansion. The second wave of expansion, unlike the first, derived from a popular conviction that higher education for its young citizens was socially, and especially economically, beneficial to a nation – sufficiently so to warrant massive public subsidization of expansion of university education. This conviction, like the concurrent and reciprocally reinforcing rise of faith in the national benefits of scientific research, was superimposed on the general tendency of increasing affluence to create both increasing economic incentives for higher education and increasing economic capacity to bear its costs. And it owed much more than was generally appreciated at the time or since to the Americans' acceptance, in their Cold War rivalry with Russia, of the achieved rate of economic growth as the key test of the competence of alternative systems of economic organization, as well as to the blow dealt to American confidence in the supremacy of American science by Russia's success in launching Sputnik in 1957.

The many problems which have been associated with the forced rapid expansion of universities in recent years are matters of too recent observation and experience to be worth detailed summary here. The most fundamental facts are, first, that university expansion has, at least temporarily, reached or exceeded a market limit set in an interdependent way by job opportunities for university graduates and students seeking university enrolment. This reaching of the limit impinges, or is in process of impinging, most heavily on graduate work, which as already mentioned is closely connected through an accelerator mechanism with the rate of expansion of undergraduate enrolments. The problem threatens to be a serious one indeed for economics departments in Canada, which have been set on a path of expansion of graduate work in an excessive number of relatively small departments which could only be realized and justified by a very large-scale expansion of the total number of qualified students seeking higher university degrees. Second, the consequences of approaching this 'natural limit' have been exacerbated by a revulsion against the universities of public and governmental opinion, based partly on disgust with the antics of students, and even more of university staff and administrators, during the period of student troubles, and based still more firmly on alarm at the mounting financial burden of supporting what again has come to be widely regarded as an over-privileged elite class of drones.

Academic politics in economics

The professionalization and expansion of economics in the post-World-War-II period and the broadening of the social origins and outlook of economists beyond the traditional origins and outlook of the previous generation have involved various kinds of strains, which I describe as 'political' in a very loose sense, within economics departments. Some manifestations of these phenomena are university-wide, and as such fall outside the scope of this paper. These include the frequent absence of real understanding of the university tradition of privileged but responsible intellectual independence for the teachers, which has underlain the willingness of significant groups of staff to condone and concur in the politization of the university. Not only have they sought to convert the university into a pressure group promoting minority political opinion on national political issues – including the application of coercive pressures for conformity to fellow scholars – but they have viewed the university quite wrongly as a self-sufficient community that should respond 'democratically' to the wishes of its 'constituency' of students, irrespective of the facts that both staff and students are supported by a public which assumes that their activities serve a useful social purpose and that students are a transient population with no responsibility for keeping the academic house in order for their successors. At a more mundane but in important respects potentially equally corruptive level, these factors among others have led to the diffusion from the applied natural sciences to the social sciences of the assumption by university staff that university employment provides a respectable address and a safe bread-and-butter income on the basis of which one is entitled to establish a commercial consulting, research, and literary enterprise. This has been one of the more legitimate focuses of student criticism (by no means exclusively 'radical') of present-day universities, though it is admittedly difficult to draw a clear line in an increasingly oral culture between outside activities that compete with and those that are complementary to good teaching and scientific research. (Other legitimate points of criticism concern course contents, which are often monuments to the eccentricities of past scholars or the intellectual eminence of other universities, and teaching methods, which frequently combine the technological primitiveness of socratic method with virtually complete absence of Socratic wisdom.)

As regards economics itself, professionalization and expansion have introduced broadly political conflict in several dimensions. The fundamental source of these conflicts is that there is a profound difference in personal and scholarly life styles between the older and the new generations of economists. At the risk of caricature, a scholar of the older generation qualified himself for academic appointment by displaying mastery of his subject through his BA written examinations, a form of test that leaves a great deal to be desired through its provision of a wide range of questions lending itself to strategic planning of study, its encouragement to brightly packaged regurgitation of material digested from lectures, and its absence of adequate testing of capacity either for genuine originality or for the sustained hard work that is almost invariably a prerequisite for genuinely original scholarly contribution. BA performance might or might not be seasoned with postgraduate study, usually not leading to a degree. Upon appointment the scholar usually picked out for himself a long-range field or topic of study, confident in the knowledge that competition would be minimal and that he would have mostly his own intellectual standards to satisfy. His teaching commitment was primarily to expose the undergraduate to the experience of seeing an older, more versatile and experienced mind at work. His scholarly commitment was almost invariably to one university in which he counted on spending his lifetime; his judges accordingly were his colleagues in that university, who not being expert in his field, judged him by personal impressions of his conversation and reading of his occasional literary productions; and the nature of his carreer allowed considerable time for assuming the responsibilities of amateur and unpaid university administration, a field in which the more ambitious university man could profitably graduate himself to professional status. Though he lived in a relatively small community, he remained somewhat detached from it.

By contrast, again at the risk of caricature, a man of the younger generation is qualified by formal graduate instruction culminating in the PhD, almost invariably undertaken at a university different from both his BA university and the university that eventually employs him. His intellectual environment is his professional discipline or his specialization within it, rather than his department and university. He tends to regard administration as a distraction from his main work and as a necessary chore to be minimized, rather than as a vital part of his life and responsibilities as he matures and a possible stepping-stone to superior status in his community. He is actively involved in the world of affairs – and not timidly so because he is a confident expert capable of delivering wanted performances, not merely a luxury of social aloofness that a busy society affords itself. The price of his different kind and degree of freedom is continuing active participation in the scholarly and research-completion process, rather than early demonstration of brilliance and continuing promise of a single great performance.

There are, of course, virtues and vices on both sides of the coin – as well as considerable misunderstanding when the two styles of scholarship became confused in the mind of the outside world, and even more so when they become confused in the mind and behaviour of the scholar himself. But I believe that the two contrasting styles of scholarship have to be viewed in the context of an evolving society waxing in affluence as a consequence of the conscious application of knowledge to the improvement of the human condition. In the perspective of history, the older style of scholarship represents the determination of a few dedicated men to preserve and painfully increase man's scarce stock of fundamental truth against the destructive pressures of cultural barbarism. It is an anachronism, or nearly so, in an age of large-scale, collective pursuit of new and usable truth by the organized and cooperative activities of a host of scholars supported by a public keenly interested in the answers.

Be that as it may – and one must bear in mind that one is not legislating compulsory conformity of all scholars to one monolithic concept of scholarship – the conflict between the older and newer styles of scholarship shows up at a variety of points in the process of academic self-government. A number of the resulting lines of political division are fairly self-evident: brightness and promise versus sustained performance as the standard for first appointment – and more importantly as the criterion for tenure and promotion, where still another criterion enters, administrative and/or teaching service to the department and the university; the debate over 'publish or perish' as a rule for academic advancement within an institution; and a variety of questions concerning departmental management, including the attention to be paid to teaching and the extent to which department members should be allowed freedom to teach what they are interested in as they want to teach it, and allocated timetable space and examination course-credits accordingly. This range of conflicts is especially acute at the level of graduate work, where the older style of scholarship tends to regard such work as an apprenticeship to be served by youth in the casual company of the old, and to be catered for by the offering of courses, and preferably of seminars, in the subjects that interest senior staff members, with standards set individually by themselves, while the new style of scholarship favours more structured courses focussing on the core of the discipline as agreed by the generality of the profession at large, with more or less uniform standards determined collectively by the department (or its senior members). This division, in turn, has far-reaching implications for standards and criteria of hiring and promotion of staff, notably for whether a department (and its university) should aim in its staff selection policies at a balanced range of high competence or at a few stellar appointments supported by a majority of mediocrities.

I myself (as already hinted) am strongly of the view that the older style of scholarship is outmoded; in particular, that contemporary universities are preparing their students for the transition from the small local environments from which they predominantly come, to competition in a broader provincial, national, or international arena, and that accordingly they should aim at providing the best possible portable training rather than one dominated by the ultimate idiosyncracies of the small group of scholars on whom they have conferred initial appointments and a virtual guarantee of tenure. This implies thinking in terms of departments of economics rather than of individual stellar economic personalities. Similarly, 'publish or perish', properly administered, seems to me a necessary corrective to the propensity of the individual scholar to hoard his knowledge against the possibility of its productive use by others and to use it to build a monopoly position with and for his own immediate students. The traditional structure and practices of universities encourage the formation of antisocial monopolies of knowledge in all sorts of ways, and these tendencies have been reinforced by the combination of public finance of universities and consequent rationing of access by faculty judgments of academic qualifications. 'Publish or perish' counteracts the influence of monopoly by forcing its products to be made available to scholars – and much more important, to students – everywhere; and it is no real restraint on the academic actively involved in the world of scholarship, for whom publication of results is necessary to the completion of research and not merely an infinitely deferrable frill on self-satisfaction or exposure of personal vanity to collegial criticism.

Nevertheless, it must be recognized that the rise of the new style of scholarship in economics represents to a significant extent the influence of two probably transitory forces. The first is the longer-run effects of the various revolutions in economics of the 1930s, which afforded the new generation a chance to over-leap the old by the exploitation of new theories and techniques which they could master more easily and at a relatively early age. The second is the recent rapid expansion of economics departments, in response to the general public desire for expanded opportunities for university education. This 'undergraduate-propelled expansion', as Professor A.D. Scott labelled it in his 1967 Presidential Address to the Canadian Political Science Association, has meant a sharp increase in the proportion of freshly-trained Ph Ds and ABDs in the average economics department, with consequent emphasis on advanced technique, more rational organization of instruction, and involvement in graduate training in the style of the major centres from which the new recruits have largely come. A slowing down in the rate of technical progress in the advance of economics itself, combined with a deceleration of the growth of demand for economists in academic institutions, may well mean a trend back towards the older style of scholarship, as a matter of accumulating wisdom through aging and experience, and the older style of treatment of graduate students, as a minor adjunct to the main job of producing good undergraduates.

Ideological influences on economic controversy
A major theme of this paper has been the professionalization of academic economics in the period since World War II, a professionalization built on the one hand on the various 'revolutions' of the 1930s and on the other hand on the great expansion of both the demand for and the supply of economists in academic and related careers. With professionalization, and in particular as a result of the intense preoccupation with the status of value judgments in economics that followed Robbins's challenge to Pigovian/utilitarian welfare economics and the subsequent concern with the empirical and quantitative study of economic matters, has come a marked decline in the attention given to

and emotional heat generated by ideological issues, in contrast particularly to the 1930s, among the mass of qualified professional economists. Economics as a subject for discussion by educated laymen, however, has always involved ideological issues, centring on moral aspects of the role of capital and of the pricing process for labour in the economic system, and professionalization of the subject has been accompanied to a significant extent by 'internalization' of some of these issues within the profession itself.

In discussing this aspect of contemporary economics, it is necessary to distinguish between the level of discourse at what might be called the marginal or rank-and-file professional level (which includes the pronouncements of or debates among some quite high-ranking economists, addressed to the rank-and-file and the outside literate intelligentsia) and controversy at the theoretical core of the subject, the latter being by far the more interesting.

At the rank-and-file level, the possession of superior economic insight has traditionally and typically been confused with the expression of plausible doubts about how far capitalism approximates some usually unspecified ideal of human perfection, by those who for one reason or another find comfort and personal identity in the expression of such doubts.[16] (I would be the first to admit, and even to assert, that the scientific approach and scientific progress depend on the expression of doubt and the demand for confirmation of alleged truth; what I refer to here, however, is making a career out of the expression of doubts as if its expression provided its own empirical confirmation.) Some of the revolutions of the 1930s provided, and continue to provide, new and more sophisticated techniques for the pursuit of this apparently respectably scientific but in fact fundamentally anti-scientific type of academic and intellectual activity. Thus the new welfare economics offered both limitless possibilities of positive or negative externalities as a reason why the competitive market system could never possibly be efficient, and the impossibility of arriving scientifically at value judgments about the desirable distribution of income as a clinching reason why competition could never possibly arrive at interpersonal justice. Moreover, by scaring away the angel-philosophers of the older utilitarianism, it created a vacuum into which any self-appointed spokesman for society's moral feelings about income distribution could happily rush. Similarly, the imperfect competition revolution provided new and more sophisticated analytical support for the long-standing ideas that profits originate merely in illegitimate monopoly privilege and serve no social function, and that the mass of the public does not know what is good for it. The alleged evidence for the former was product differentiation and for the latter commercial advertising – though both phenomena are far more evident, and far more evidently socially costly, in the political rather than in the commercial realm. (Far more people have been consistently much more taken in by promises of something for nothing, or of satisfaction beyond all price, through the purchase of a cheap and commonplace product offered by politicians than by promises of the same sort made by the manufacturers of soap – soap at least makes you cleaner and less obnoxious to your fellow human beings, whatever it may or may not do for your psyche.) Finally, the Keynesian revolution, with its residual policy assumption that the capitalist system ought to be capable of delivering at all times a politically determined minimum percentage of unemployment within an equally politically determined tolerable maximum rate of inflation, usually equated with zero, was widely interpreted as setting the seal of scientific legitimacy on a standard of performance impossible for any economic system to fulfil. (It also sanctified two much longer-standing tenets of radical belief: that the self-seeking activities of monopolies of labour have social legitimacy denied with loathing to monopolies based on capital or industrial knowledge, and that society possesses vast reservoirs of resources which only the stupidity or self-seeking of the capitalists prevents from being used for noble social purposes.)

Superficialities of this kind are remarkable only for their capacity to seduce self-respecting and otherwise reasonable and educated people and perhaps to demonstrate that P.T. Barnum's dictum that 'there's a sucker born every minute' is a masterpiece of understatement. Fairness requires one to acknowledge, however, that there are plenty of dogmatists on the other side of the argument who refuse to meditate on matters such as the influence of inheritance and the inefficiencies of the educational and legal systems on the actual distribution of opportunities for self-betterment among individuals who appear to be equally placed.

Far more interesting, from both a scientific-professional and a social point of view, is the fierce controversy that has been raging at a high level, between the arcane pure theorists of Cambridge, England, and Cambridge, Massachusetts, no less, to distinguish two identically named institutional locations by their respective intellectual provinces, over the nature of capital and the role of capital and the production function in the theory of distribution. This controversy centres on the rediscovery by Joan Robinson, of Cambridge, England, that capital, being a man-made embodiment of original resources in machinery and structures, cannot in strict logic be treated as an easily quantifiable input into a production function, and that distribution of income therefore cannot (at the same level) be regarded as determined by the quantity of capital relative to labour. This general point has since become embodied in the specific proposition that the rate of return on capital is not an unique monotonically decreasing function of the quantity of capital, a point originally treated as an exceptional case, 'the Ruth Cohen case', in Robinson's *The Accumulation of Capital*, but since come to be dignified as 'the reverse switching problem'.[17]

Had the reverse switching problem been discovered by someone other than the high priestess at Keynes's shrine in Cambridge, it would in all probability have wound up as a short journal article, or even been left in its original form as a possible but empirically uninteresting exceptional case pointed out by a bright junior colleague, to be duly noted but otherwise ignored by conscientious scholars thereafter. Instead, in the hands of Joan Robinson and her followers, it has become the final convincing demonstration that capitalism cannot possibly work, 'orthodox' or traditional mainstream economics is a bunch of nonsense, and socialism as both an alternative economic system and an emotional protest against capitalism is the only viable alternative.

This sweeping claim reflects the rudimentary and confused state of economics in the 1930s from which the basic ideas involved spring, and is in an important sense a counter-revolution against the validated revolutions that have occurred in economics since that time rather than the radical revolution in economic thought it claims to be. First, the choice of the aggregate prodution function and the older, more literary theories of distribution that preceded it and remained its penumbra reflects the very early stages of the introduction of mathematical methods into economics, in the form of Douglas's joint invention and empirical application of the Cobb-Douglas production function and Hicks's use of the aggregate production function and the elasticity of substitution to tackle classical Ricardian problems of distribution theory in his *The Theory of Wages*.[18] (Joan Robinson was herself involved in the long intellectual straining to understand the elasticity of substitution that filled the pages of *The Review of Economic Studies* in its early years.) A single aggregate production function necessarily makes the distribution of income depend technologically on relative factor quantities and the technology shaping the production function, to the exclusion of both the demand factors that Marshall taught economists to emphasize at the micro-economic level and the questions of morality, monopoly power, etc. that concern the critic of capitalism. But such an aggregate production function is a transitional stage to a general equilibrium analysis of a many-sector model. From this analysis it becomes evident both that it may not be possible to construct a 'surrogate' aggregate production function and that nothing important depends on whether one can do so or not – a point with which theorists of capital in the classical tradition were quite familiar.

Leaving aside the possibility of multiple equilibrium, which in no other economic context would be held to be fatal either to economic analysis or to capitalism, the distribution of income is perfectly determinate on marginal productivity principles within a general equilibrium model incorporating demand factors. The assertion that the contrary is true is this generation's Cambridge (England) myth. Joan Robinson supports it sometimes by relying on the imperfect competition theory view that profit is determined by monopoly power and sometimes by reference to the short-run, Great-Depression-oriented Keynesian view that savings and investment do not tend to equality at full employment. Her colleague Piero Sraffa[19] supports this view by constructing a brilliant precursor of the modern linear-programming theory of production in which relative prices depend only on the real wage rate or the interest rate, and by refusing to attempt to explain the interest rate except by a vague reference to liquidity preference. Their colleague Nicholas Kaldor[20] goes them one better by accepting the premise that capitalism works, but maintaining that the reason cannot be anything so simple as that provided by the classical theoretical tradition. Instead, in his view, it requires two new theories: a Keynesian theory of income distribution to replace marginal productivity theory, and a Kaldorian theory of technical progress to make the rate of capital accumulation entrepreneurs want consistent with the rate of population growth.

In the second place, the underlying methodology of the Joan Robinson exercise reflects the fallacious methodology popularized by the imperfect competition revolution, itself the outcome of much work in the 1920s on the question of what Marshall and his contemporaries meant by the assumption of 'perfect competition', and subsequently by the welfare economics revolution. This methodology rested on the belief that one can dispose of a theory by finding an error in its logic or a lack of 'realism' in its assumptions. (Note that this same belief motivates Marx's attack on the 'classical school' of English economics.) That belief is false: the contemporarily accepted methodology of positive economics maintains that one can falsify a theory only by falsifying its predictions.[21] By that test, no amount of logic-chopping designed to show that capitalism is impossible in pure theory can dispose of the fact that capitalism actually exists and actually works and has worked fairly well as a system for most of its history, the major exception occuring in the Great Depression of 1929 and after when the recuperative powers of the system were insufficient to overcome the crisis imposed by gross national and international monetary mismanagement.

Third, in line with the Kaleckian version of the Keynesian theory,[22] the renewed interest in capital and growth, stimulated but by no means entirely aroused by Joan Robinson's work, has thrown modern theory, in spite of or perhaps because of the extreme sophistication of its treatment of the production side of the economy, back into the crude Marxist model (cruder, it may be noted, than the preceding Ricardian model, which allowed for rents earned by sheer scarcity) of an economic system employing only two factors of production – homogeneous labour and capital – identified with two social classes – workers' and 'capitalists' – distinguished by different average propensities to save.

In view of the theoretically, methodologically, and sociologically reactionary nature of the model involved and the deliberate sacrifice of much intellectually hard-won understanding of the economic system that its use entails, the interesting scientific question is why this particular controversy has excited so much theoretical attention and absorbed the time and effort of so many able theorists, especially the younger students of the subject. One obvious reason is the success of the mathematical/general equilibrium revolution, which requires no knowledge of the history of economic thought, even of mathematical economics itself, and imposes no obligation to establish social relevance, beyond a plausible assertion, documented if possible, that some reputable economist has uttered a mathematical error which science requires should be cleared up. Unfortunately, with sufficient determination the clearing up process can always be shown to have created further messes requiring further clearing up, and so on *ad infinitum.*

A more interesting explanatory factor, with broader implications, concerns the politics of institutional leadership and institutional rivalry for leadership. In very sketchy outline, the pre-eminence of Cambridge, England in economics achieved at the end of the 1930s, largely due to Keynes's *General Theory*, both enabled Keynes's successors to exploit Cambridge's prestige for the propagation of their own political beliefs (which were vastly different from Keynes's own), and attracted to Cambridge a continuing stream of able students. The able student's optimal career strategy, assuming the normal degree of risk aversion, is to go to the best place available and try to distinguish himself by doing what scholars there think should be done. By so doing, students both advance their own careers and serve the institution by becoming devoted proselytizers for the true faith among the heathen from whose ranks they sprang. At the same time, the pre-eminence of Cambridge, England, accepted by Harvard University, Massachusetts as a result of the conquest of that institution by the Keynesian revolution, offered the newly established department of the Massachusetts Institute of Technology an opportunity to spring to prominence over Harvard in the United States profession by challenging Cambridge, England, on its chosen ground of pure theory. Thus Cambridge, England, became a punching bag for MIT; and, if one may be permitted to personalize a punching bag, it continued to consider itself a champion because it could never be dislodged from its initial position and occasionally struck back when the real champion missed a punch through over-confidence. Students taught by a punching bag are very unlikely to question their teacher's assessment of who is winning the fight, let alone learn what the fight is about or how to rate a fighter properly.

Furthermore, to abandon the boxing metaphor abruptly and turn to broader international political considerations, the post-World-War-II period has been characterized until relatively very recently by the international political and economic dominance of the United States, and in economics itself by the somewhat vulgarly ebullient dominance of the American scientific approach. In the meantime, the United Kingdom has been dwindling in importance in the world economy, and losing or throwing away the international prestige gained by a graceful abandonment of the erstwhile British empire, to the point where economic integration with Europe has become the last available desperate gamble on reversing the downward trend. This process of apparently inexorable decline has occurred in spite of the self-assumed superiority of British over foreign economics, derived to a not inconsiderable extent from the strong socialist and nationalist leanings inherited from the intellectual and political turmoil of the 1920s and 1930s; in fact, this inheritance has meant in practice that at every point of crucial economic policy decision British economics has reacted either with political dogma or with political opportunism. Under the circumstances, it is understandable that a developing and increasingly despairing national inferiority complex should have expressed itself in an attempt at the intellectual level to dispose of United States hegemony by ostensibly purely scientific debate about the intellectual foundations of the American economic system, and,– as so often happens in such matters – that the intellectual weakness of the challenge should have been disguised by stridency of assertion of propositions and by an unrelenting quest among the counter-arguments of the challenged for firmer and more plausible grounds for dispute. It is equally understandable, though no less pitiable, that intellectuals professing economics in other countries with less objectively justified but emotionally equally strong leanings towards anti-Americanism should have seized on the challenge initiated by Cambridge, England, as an apparently pure scientific rallying-point for their anti-Americanism; and specifically, that Joan Robinson should have become the folk-heroine of the American radical minority, much of the Italian economics profession, and certain economics departments in east-central Canada.

As recorded in an earlier section, the profession of economics in Canada has shared in the general tendency towards the professionalization of the subject consequent on the various revolutions in economics of the 1930s and other factors previously mentioned. One would expect a continuing improvement in the quality of professional work in the subject in Canada, especially as rising affluence is likely to strengthen the social and economic independence of the academic community, and as demographic changes of various kinds gradually erode the traditional position of Canadian academics as a privileged class kept safe from the harsh conditions of life in a pioneering community by the reciprocated support of a White Anglo-Saxon Protestant elite. There are, however, certain factors which may make actual performance fall short of potential.

First, the Canadian economics community – with the notable brilliant exception of Harold Adams Innis – has always been, by a very wide margin, a net importer of economic theory. Indeed, if it were not for the prolonged sojourn here of John Rae in the early nineteenth century, historians of economic thought in Canada would have nothing but gossip to write until well into the post-World-War-I period. The problem is that, under the impact of the mathematical economics and general equilibrium analysis revolutions and the basically political controversy between the two Cambridges which has dominated the theoretical field, the fundamental core subject of micro-economics on which the rest of economics depends for its strength has moved far away from the simple but solid bed-rock of comprehensible principles laid down by the English classics and neo-classics out into the deeps of elaborate formal model construction. In consequence, it takes a much better mind to master it, and a still better mind to teach students why it is necessary to master it and how it should be used. The evident danger is that theory in Canada will become concentrated on a super-structure of elaborate technique acquired from the best institutions in other larger countries and therefore from the most narrowly specialized and recondite sources, a superstructure suitable only for deployment in a few arcane debates at the most abstract level of pure theory and unsupported by an infrastructure of usable elementary theory meeting the needs and capacities of the everyday applied economist.

This danger is accentuated by the very thin spreading of academic effort over a large number of universities that has resulted from policy decisions regarding higher education in Canada in the past decade, which constitutes a second problem. Academic dispersion has the potentially favourable effect of undermining the monopoly position of the old established universities and imposing competitive pressures for academic excellence. But this effect will probably take from a generation to a half-century of effort and growth to bring to fruition; and in the meantime the apparent unpopularity of universities among both the public and its government – a phenomenon, it should be noted, which has emerged everywhere in the English-speaking world in the wake of excessively optimistic and expensive university expansion – may well turn diffusion of academic institutions and effort into a source of weakness rather than strength and restore and even augment the dominance of the old established universities. A particular problem in this connection concerns graduate work in economics, where there is considerable danger that the inevitable frustration of excessively optimistic plans for departmental improvement based on the development of graduate work to the PhD level will, in combination with political and institutional emphasis on 'fair shares' in the distribution of a limited pie, result in a plethora of high-cost and educationally inferior graduate programs.

The problem just mentioned is, on its purely academic side (as distinct from its financial side), in large part attributable to the prevalence in Canada of the traditional principles of university organization and remuneration, that is roughly equal pay across departments and institutions, graded by rank and more basically by seniority, together with the principle of tenure. These give the older established universities a tremendous competitive adantage over the more recently established ones, even when the newer ones are expanding rapidly enough to be able to overbid the older ones in terms of the professional opportunities they can offer to staff. Tenure, and promotion in status and pay largely by seniority, also foster the Canadian academic vices of not working hard enough and of retiring from real work early on the strength of one early bout of hard work spent on the winning of a Ph D. The prospects of development of an active and lively professional economics of world competitive status in Canada would be considerably improved if remuneration were more closely geared to sustained scholarly output and tenure were granted much more sparingly. It may be noted that both competition for quality of staff, and financial stringency, have been pushing at least a few Canadian universities in this direction.

Finally, perhaps the most serious threat to the prospects of continuing progress in the development of professional economics in Canada is the possibility of implementation of nationalist demands to confine graduate work in Canada to Canadian citizen students and academic posts in Canada to citizen graduates of Canadian universities. The high quality of Canadian undergraduate instruction in economics, for which the country remains justifiably internationally famous – though that reputation may not survive the effects of the implementation of student demands for the 'democratization' (so-called) of undergraduate instruction – has been built on the willingness and indeed anxiety of Canadian universities to obtain the best teaching staff they could from wherever they could get it, though subject to a natural though not always efficiency-promoting preference for Canadians, other things being equal. At the present stage of development of Canadian economics, an overt preference for Canadian citizens or prospective citizens in appointments to academic posts would probably not be too harmful, though it would certainly not be positively helpful, to the ultimate social objective – which is or ought to be to provide the best possible training for Canadian students, not a monopoly of university jobs for Canadian-citizen teachers. But given the generally low quality of graduate training in economics in Canadian universities – a consequence of small scale of operation and primary concentration on undergraduate instruction – insistence on Canadian training of Canadian university staff would guarantee the intellectual impoverishment of Canadian students in almost all Canadian universities as well as conferring an undeserved and unwarranted monopoly power over Canadian economics on the old established universities in central Canada. This would indeed be a heavy social price to pay to safeguard Canadian intellectuals from the risk of contamination by competition in the world intellectual market place.

NOTES

1 For a more extensive treatment, see Harry G. Johnson, *The Theory of Income Distribution* (Gray-Mills, 1973), especially chapters 1-3
2 Alfred Marshall, *Principles of Economics*, ninth ed. (Macmillan for the Royal Economic Society, 1961)
3 A.C. Pigou, *The Economics of Welfare* (Macmillan, 1920)
4 Joan Robinson, *The Economics of Imperfect Competition* (Macmillan, 1933); also Edward H. Chamberlin, *The Theory of Monopolistic Competition* (Harvard, 1933)
5 For an account of the development of thinking on this problem, see P.A. Samuelson, 'The Monopolistic Competition Revolution,' *Monopolistic Competition Theory: Studies in Impact*, R.E. Kuennel, ed. (John Wiley and Sons, 1967), chapter 4, pp.105-38
6 Lionel Robbins, *The Nature and Significance of Economic Science* (Macmillan, 1932)
7 See especially J.R. Hicks, *Value and Capital* (Oxford, 1939)
8 J.M. Keynes, *The General Theory of Employment, Interest and Money* (Macmillan, 1936)
9 See P.A. Samuelson, *Foundations of Economic Analysis* (Harvard, 1947), chapter 7, p.250, where it is remarked that to insist on the conditions for production and exchange optimization while refusing to make interpersonal comparisons 'is like saying that it does not matter whether or not a man has hair, so long as it is curly'
10 Kenneth J. Arrow, *Social Choice and Individual Values*, Cowles Commission for Research in Economics Monograph 12 (John Wiley and Sons, 1951)
11 J.E. Meade, *The Theory of International Economic Policy*, vol. II, *Trade and Welfare* (Oxford, 1955); also R.G. Lipsey and K.J. Lancaster, 'The General Theory of Second Best,' *Review of Economic Studies*, XXIV (1956-57), pp.11-32
12 R.H. Coase, 'The Problem of Social Cost,' *Journal of Law and Economics*, III (October 1960), pp.1-44
13 Anthony Downs, *An Economic Theory of Democracy*, (Harper and Row, 1957); see also Albert Breton, *The Economic Theory of Representative Democracy* (Aldine-Atherton, 1974, forthcoming)
14 See Harry G. Johnson, 'Recent Developments in Monetary Theory,' *Essays in Monetary Economics* (Allen & Unwin, 1967), chapter 2; also 'The Keynesian Revolution and the Monetarist Counter-Revolution,' *American Economic*

Review, LXI (May 1971), pp.1-14, reprinted in H.G. Johnson, *Further Essays in Monetary Economics* (Allen & Unwin, 1973) chapter 2

15 See Harry G. Johnson, "The Monetary Approach to Balance-of-Payments Theory,' *International Trade and Money*, M.B. Connolly and A.K. Swoboda, eds. (Allen & Unwin, 1972), chapter 11, pp.206-23, reprinted in Harry G. Johnson, *Further Essays in Monetary Economics*, chapter 9

16 Economics at this level has been brilliantly written on by John Kenneth Galbraith in *The Affluent Society* (Houghton Mifflin, 1957), and *The New Industrial State* (Houghton Mifflin, 1967). From another point of view, Galbraith is the only leading contemporary economist to apply Marx's method seriously to modern society, as contrasted with interpreting modern society in outdated emotive language, by analysing the contemporary system of production.

17 Joan Robinson, *The Accumulation of Capital* (Macmillan, 1956); for a Cambridge-oriented view of the controversy, see G.C. Harcourt, 'Some Cambridge Controversies in the Theory of Capital,' *Journal of Economic Literature*, VII (June 1969), pp.369-405

18 Paul H. Douglas, *Theory of Wages* (New York: Macmillan Co., 1934), also J.R. Hicks, *The Theory of Wages* second ed. (Macmillan, 1963)

19 Piero Sraffa, *Production of Commodities by Means of Commodities* (Cambridge, 1960)

20 Nicholas Kaldor, 'Alternative Theories of Distribution,' *Review of Economic Studies*, XXIII (1956), pp.83-100

21 Milton Friedman, 'The Methodology of Positive Economics,' *Essays in Positive Economics* (Chicago, 1953), part II, p.251

22 Michael Kalecki, *Selected Essays on the Dynamics of the Capitalist Economy* (Cambridge, 1971), chapters 1-3

Commentary M.F. GOODCHILD

The campus newspaper ran an article on this conference on Tuesday in which the author noted that Dr Johnson's paper would be followed by remarks from two commentators from other departments in the Faculty of Social Science, who would 'display their knowledge of economics'. I was struck by the author's telling insight into my own plight as a geographer. I have a strong mental image of the paper we have just heard. I understand the beginning, in which it is argued that economics in Canada must be seen as one section of a fairly homogeneous, world-wide whole; and I understand the end, in which we return to an assessment of specifically Canadian prospects; but of the middle I can make neither head nor tail. I see the paper rather as a wartime picture of a bombed and shattered bridge. The ends are hanging from the banks, but the middle is invisible, sunk beneath what to me at least is very muddy water. Somewhere in there is someone called Joan Robinson.

You began, sir, with a dichotomy. Before World War I the discipline was divided on geographical lines. There was the British school, the Austrian, the Italian, and so on. You argued that many social sciences might still see themselves in this nation-state context today, because of geographically specific subject matter. But contemporary divisions in economics are upon philosophical and methodological, not territorial grounds. Economics has become aspatial.

I cannot see geography falling neatly into either category. Some geographers are international in outlook, paying as much attention to developments in Europe and Asia as they do to those in the North-American literature. The work of others is continental, national, or even provincial in scope. The spectrum is very closely linked to that from purist to applied. The work of many practical geographers in resource management is so linked to aspects of public policy as to be virtually untransportable.

This classification on the basis of scale is also highly dynamic. Efforts at environmental improvement, which were initially made at a very local level, are slowly increasing in scope. We now demand for all of our citizens a ubiquitous environmental quality which at one time only the wealthy could afford for their immediate surroundings. As we move from provincial to continental problems it becomes increasingly evident that the last, most difficult and challenging tasks will be at the global level, if only from the Second Law of Thermodynamics.

You saw the old nation-state organization of the discipline as essentially artificial, maintained by differences in language and culture, the need for each national school to interpret the particular local stage of industrial development, and difficulties in communication and travel. Contemporary economics is international largely because the transmission of ideas is now so rapid, and because professionals can flit from school to school in our contracting global village with the ease of butterflies. But just as travel facilitates homogenization, it also facilitates sorting out. Intellectual minorities which were previously so dispersed as to be incoherent can now muster together. One might well see the academic community as becoming more geographically concentrated, rather than more dispersed. But neither of these alternatives can make much impact on the observed tendency for the academic community to be spatially organized to minimize local competition, to place one representative of each field in each department.

I have two reactions, then, as a geographer. The first is to the evident importance of geographical factors in the development of a discipline – the geography of economic science if you like. The second is to try to follow your initial distinction as it applies to my own discipline, and I find that rather than a dichotomy, there is a continuum of scale in outlook and organization. Following from this last point, I would like to end these rather brief comments with a direct question.

I can see that if you had decided that economics was still a nation-state discipline, your conclusions and recommendations would be basically similar: the profession would best be served by fostering academic competition, granting tenure sparingly, and evaluating on sustained performance rather than early promise. But what if both views were necessary in a single department? Would the same conclusions apply both to a diverse department with a variety of philosophies, and to the case of a mature, unified discipline with a unidimensional goal?

Commentary C.B. MACPHERSON

We are all prisoners of our discipline, to a greater or lesser extent. We are so simply because we must, in order to practise a discipline, start from its assumptions and its characteristic ways of thinking; and because the incentives to stay within them, or the disincentives to depart from them, are quite strong. The degree of confinement may vary, from close imprisonment to merely house arrest. As a general rule I think we may say that the degree of imprisonment depends on, and varies directly with, the degree of refinement of the discipline: the more refined, the more subtle, the discipline is, the closer the confinement. The work of the medieval schoolmen is the most obvious illustration of this principle.

No one doubts that of all the social sciences economics is now the most refined. And Professor Johnson's depiction of the present state of economics is an admirable illustration of the law that confinement varies directly with refinement. Indeed one wonders if the apparent causal relation should not be reversed. On the surface, the confinement appears to be the result of the refinement. But perhaps it is the other way around: perhaps it is that economics has indulged in refinement in order to stay within a self-imposed confinement, to stay within a narrow vision of an economy as detached as possible from society.

That, at least, is what is suggested by Professor Johnson's assessment of the superiority of neo-classical over classical economics: the main change from classical to neo-classical, he sees, I think correctly, as the move away from the classical interest in the distribution of the whole social product among social classes, or the abandonment of the classical identification of the shares going to the factors of production (land, labour and capital) with the income shares of the classes which owned them (landowners, workers and capitalists). This was indeed a change. But why is it regarded as an advance? Is it more realistic to attend to class contributions to production and class shares of the product (as the classical economists did) or to drop this approach in favour of 'a unified theory of the logic of choice based on application of the principle of marginalism to consumer choice among commodities and producer choice among factors of production' (as the neo-classicals have done)? The neo-classicals' claim to realism − to their model representing the actual economy more accurately than the previous or any alternative model − is at least suspect, involving, as it does, treating consumers individually or in the aggregate as sovereign, treating producers (of all sizes) as compelled by the logic of the market to make their choices serve the choices of the consumers; or (which doesn't seem quite consistent with consumer sovereignty) treating the aggregate of producers (of all sizes) and the aggregate of consumers (of all sizes) as equal forces in the markets both for products and factors of production. The logic of choice, undifferentiated by class, replaces the logic of class.

But surely, as long as we have classes, which means at least as long as we have a recognizably capitalist economy (which is, after all, what the neo-classical theory purports to explain) it is not very realistic to abstract entirely from classes. To do so is about as realistic as it is to abstract from the characteristics of capital in a capitalist economy so far as to define the primitive hunter's bow and arrow as capital, an approach often taken in elementary textbooks in economics, and adopted even by those who should know better, like A.A. Berle in his recent book on *Power*.[1] They should know better, but they don't because they are prisoners – happy prisoners –of 'a unified theory of the logic of choice'.

Professor Johnson distinguishes three schools of contemporary economics. The first is 'scientific economics, the application of logic and quantitative methods to the understanding, interpretation and production of economic phenomena': this is the current refinement – a largely mathematical refinement – of neo-classical economics. The second is Marxist economics, about which he has nothing but shrill ill to say. The third is 'developmental' economics, which, he says, resembles 'the pre-scientific mercantilist stage of the evolution of economic theory, most notably in its espousal of all sorts of governmental economic interventions as the only possible means of building an economically powerful nation-state'. If it were not for one tart remark Professor Johnson makes about Milton Friedman, one would conclude from this catalogue that Professor Johnson had sunk to the very depths of Chicago 'laissez-faire'. I am happy to see that he has not sunk quite so far. But he has apparently committed himself to the proposition that there is one scientific economics – 'the unified theory of the logic of choice' – which can be scientific only by abstracting both from class differentia and from the national concerns of the political economy of the underdeveloped nations, whose first concern must obviously be to build an economically viable nation-state. I find this a rather odd position to be taken by one who pays such tribute to the Innis tradition of political economy. It is true that Innis was reluctant to recognize the role of class, but with respect to underdeveloped countries he was surely the most perceptive Canadian-nationalist political economist.

I can only conclude that Professor Johnson's doubts about the prospects of economics in Canada would be fully justified if one could allow his assumption about what constitutes scientific economics. If his assumption were correct, Canadian economics would, almost certainly, be kept permanently in a satellite position. Now I do not share the view expressed occasionally that Professor Johnson wishes to reduce Canada, or Canadian economics, to a satellite position. But if he had wished to do so he could not have taken a line more likely to have that result. The abandonment of political economy is, at the present juncture, tantamount to the undermining of economics in Canada.

NOTE

1 Cf. C.B. Macpherson, 'Bow and Arrow Power,' *The Nation*, 210 (19 January 1970), pp.54-6.

4
History: the invertebrate social science

There must be occasions, even in this day and age, when the historians of the University of Western Ontario wonder about the appropriateness of their accommodation in a social science building. Certainly if no such unease exists, then this university must have one of the very few groups of historians who have concluded, finally, that their natural habitat is among the social scientists rather than among the humanists. But even if the historians have banished their last qualm about deserting their old humanistic mistress in favour of co-habitation with a new technologically ample goddess, there must certainly be those among the economists, psychologists, geographers and other assorted model-builders, card-punchers and survey-takers who still wonder what right historians have to enter their socially scientific temple. Surely it was not so long ago that historians everywhere were heard dutifully intoning parts of W.H. Auden's Decalogue:

Thou shalt not answer questionnaires
Or quizzes upon World Affairs,
Nor with compliance
Take any test. Thou shalt not sit
With statisticians nor commit
A social science.

Whether the last doubts of the true social scientists have been entirely dissipated is for others to judge. But it is surely true that few historians, any longer, would refuse to 'commit a social science'. Still it must also be admitted, hastily, that the good historian, as distinct from a mere technician, can never wholly reject his humanistic heritage. That can never be exchanged for a mess of value-free social science pottage. Nor is the explanation either sentimental or merely snobbish. For the historian literacy and style are more than matters of successful communication. Unscientific as it may sound, language and style are part of the very essence of the historian's craft. So, at the outset, I must take my stand with those who believe that the historian's form of communication is 'more like that employed in the fictive arts than that employed in the sciences'.[1] The language of the historian must do more than describe with cold accuracy; it must also evoke a perceived mood. If that separates the historian from other social scientists, and I am far from certain that it does, then that element of separation should be maintained.

While most modern historians would accept an increasingly close, even a symbiotic, relationship with social scientists, there remain some disputes about the terms of the relationship. For a historian like E.H. Carr no fundamental distinction between historians and other social scientists is necessary. 'Scientists, social scientists and historians,' Carr has written, 'are all engaged in different branches of the same study: the study of man and his environment, of the effects of man on his environment, and of his environment on man. The object of the study is the same: to increase man's understanding of, and mastery over, his environment.'[2] To that confident assertion many, perhaps most, historians would reply with G.R. Elton that since only historians deal with the past from 'the point of view of happening, of change and the particular' their discipline is autonomous rather than just another social science.[3] This is an old argument, or perhaps chestnut would be a better description, about history as art or science. It is perhaps best left to undergraduate debating societies, or to those more qualified to discuss the philosophy of science, the problem of the uniqueness of historical events, the logic of historical discourse and numerous other knotty conundrums.[4] In practice, at least for historians, the problem rarely arises and is even more rarely faced.[5] The reason is not philosophical obtuseness, though doubtless some of that exists, but rather that historians have long practised a successful form of intellectual imperialism: while maintaining the autonomy of their own discipline they have been able to reach out and acquire the techniques devised by others for gathering information or formulating hypotheses about the past. There is in this sense, then, no real point in arguing about the value of the social sciences to history because, in J.H. Hexter's words, 'the application to the historical enterprise of any viable new technique for knowing is always desirable and is conditional only on the mastery of the technique and the identification of historical problems to which it can be usefully applied.'[6] History retains its autonomy – but so do economics, sociology, geography and politics.

There is a point in Hexter's comment that, despite its obviousness, deserves emphasis: the matter of mastering the technique. Nothing is more pathetic than the work of the historian who has just discovered Freud, or to whom it has recently been revealed that a computer can count. These half-discoveries rarely add anything but confusion to our understanding of the past. But even mastery of technique is valueless, perhaps even dangerous, unless the historian has trained judgment. Too often the methodology becomes the message. No amount of technical know-how can make a bad historian into a good one, since, as one advocate of greater application of social science techniques to historical studies has remarked, 'quantitative findings do not by themselves provide answers to general questions of interpretation.'[7]

That is obvious. What should be equally obvious is that social science techniques, especially those of quantification and measurement, can allow historians to make more accurate generalization by making accessible the kinds of evidence that have been nearly impossible to manage in the past. But neither these techniques, nor the new evidence that they educe, negate the value of traditional sources and techniques. Letters, newspapers, sermons, novels, painting, architecture – these sources still provide indispensible evidence of the texture of past societies, and even suggest the types of questions which should be asked about quantifiable data. 'Religion, ideology, cultural traditions,' writes Stephan Thernstrom, one of the ablest practitioners of the new urban history, 'these affected human behavior in the past and shaped the meaning of the demographic and ecological patterns which can be neatly plotted on a map or graph.'[8] Traditional evidence, even of the most impressionistic kind, is necessary not only to reveal value systems, but even to determine the meaning of some of the categories necessary in quantification: class, occupation, status and the like.

My main contention, then, is that the historian has much to learn from the social sciences, but that he will still do his job best if he continues to insist upon his own separate, but equal, identity. That identity, however, can never be unchanging and inflexible. The strength of the historical discipline, and also perhaps its weakness, has always resided in its capacity to utilize new knowledge and new methods of acquiring knowledge. In that sense history is an invertebrate discipline:[9] it lacks a backbone which would make it rigid and consequently incapable of absorbing the more highly structured and theoretical social sciences. Yet that analogy may be unfortunate, since lack of backbone bears certain moral connotations which do not fit my conception of history. It might, therefore, be safer to resort to another biological analogy. The historical discipline is a marsupial, provided by nature with a pouch in which to carry its young – the other social sciences – which are born imperfect.

Since the beaver is not a marsupial it is obviously, and mercifully, time to drop the biological analogy entirely as I turn to an examination of the uses of the social sciences in the analysis of the Canadian past.

In Canada, it might be argued, history has always been the predominant social science. The apparent arrogance of that claim will perhaps be mitigated by explaining that the historical approach has been used effectively by nearly all of the practitioners of social science in Canada. Our most distinguished sociologists, Léon Gérin and C.A. Dawson for example, always emphasized the historical dimension in their studies of social development. S.D. Clark, John Porter and Fernand Dumont, among contemporaries, work within a similar tradition. Adam Shortt, Errol Bouchette, O.D. Skelton, and Edouard Montpetit, all were political economists, but their work, like that of successors such as Norman Ward, C.B. Macpherson, James Eayrs, Léon Dion and Gérard Bergeron, was enriched through an understanding of historical materials. And perhaps no single person better epitomizes the ideal Canadian social scientist than Harold Adams Innis, an economist who wrote some of the most important and influential books in the field of Canadian history.[10] The point need hardly be further laboured: the history of Canada has been written, to a very considerable extent, by people whose professional interests combined history and social science. Historical writing in Canada has benefited enormously from this co-operation. Perhaps other social scientists would assess the benefits and costs differently, for in recent times there has been a noticeable turning away from the historical, and towards the behavioural, approach in the other disciplines. That strikes me as a not unmixed blessing, but in the meantime historians have maintained a strong social-science orientation, and it seems to be growing even stronger today. It is that orientation which, at least in part, explains the quite impressive developments that are in evidence in contemporary Canadian historical studies.

In purely quantitative terms historical studies represent a very significant proportion of the total scholarly activity in Canada today. The figures which I am about to present do not represent anything like an adequate survey. Nor is my methodology unimpeachable, being governed by the grab-bag principle of taking the data where you can most conveniently get them. Still, the intent is serious and the result does reveal some interesting facts and trends. First, at the level of graduate work, the register of postgraduate dissertations in history and related subjects show a fourfold increase in the number of theses written between 1968 and 1972 – an increase from about 500 to some 1900. Those figures cannot be taken at face value since the compilation has improved vastly in recent years and simply by becoming more inclusive would produce greater numbers. Still, it is an interesting rough measure of growth. Equally interesting, though more impressionistic, is the sense one gets of an increasing variety in the type of work being done. While there is much that is still narrowly traditional, fields like urban, labour and immigration history are growing.[11]

A second measure, again an extremely rough one, is books published. Since 1967 over 500 books which can, in some manner, be catalogued as historical have been published. I am indebted for this information to Professor Carl Berger who comments drily that 'one has the impression that no worthwhile manuscripts have remained unpublished.' A less subtle, and less charitable, writer might have made the same point more strongly. Certainly not all social scientists, or even historians would be impressed with every title. But a list which includes Andrew Clark's *Acadia: The Geography of Early Nova Scotia* and C.P. Stacey's *Arms, Men and Governments*, to say nothing of the obviously interdisciplinary *Christmas Mumming in Newfoundland: Essays in Anthropology, Folklore and History*, cannot fail, at least, to reveal the breadth of Canadian scholarly activities.[12]

To book publishing must be added the journals where new work, and new kinds of work, should find the first audience. The historians have always been well served in Canada by such national periodicals as the *Canadian Historical Review*, the *Revue d'histoire de l'amérique française*, and by local quarterlies such as *Saskatchewan History* and *Ontario History*. Naturally these publications have their times of trouble, but they continue to print a fairly high proportion of original and revisionist material. Perhaps more significant is the appearance of new journals. There are several of these and the sceptic might explain this development merely by the growth of the profession and the pressure to 'publish or perish'. Nor would anyone totally discount such explanations. But several of the journals, at least, were founded to meet new needs, and to encourage novel approaches that seemed lacking in the older, established publications. For the most part the goal of these new journals has been to develop interdisciplinary studies. *The Journal of Canadian Studies*, now in its seventh year, is open to all students of Canadian life, irrespective of discipline. In Quebec, *Recherches sociographiques*, now more than a decade old, has done much to bring historians into the company of other social scientists, and it provides some evidence of greater cross-fertilization in Quebec than has taken place in English-speaking Canada. Two regional reviews, *BC Studies* and *Acadiensis* have also attempted, with some success, to stimulate multidisciplinary analysis of regional historical subjects. Finally, mention should be made of *Social History/Histoire sociale*, which is explicitly concerned with that sector of historical study where the social sciences and their techniques are of most relevance. Along with these journals, an increasing number of interdisciplinary regional studies conferences have been launched. The most successful of these is probably the Western Canadian Studies Conference, meeting annually at Calgary, whose program includes work from every academic discipline, focusing on western Canada as its area of investigations. It is a high quality conference, as demonstrated by the papers published in *Prairie Perspectives.*[13]

No one would claim total success for all, or even perhaps any, of these new ventures. Too often the interdisciplinary journal turns out to be nothing more than one where members of various disciplines do their own thing between the covers of the same periodical. But sharing the same covers, as even non-social-scientists have long been aware, is a time-honoured way to begin a fruitful relationship.

One final way to measure the activities of historians should not be neglected – the matter of financial support. The data here is again less than exhaustive: it is only a one-year sample, but it is the latest information. The source is the *15th Annual Report* of the Canada Council for the period 1971-2. In each of three granting categories the historians find themselves well favoured. In the doctoral fellowships competition, history students stand behind only English literature in the number of candidates and the total amount of awards. ($1,307,600 for English, $1,193,300 for history). Psychology follows in third place ($914,400), after which comes political science ($836,700), economics ($781,800), sociology ($758,900), anthropology ($352,000), and geography ($233,000). In leave and research fellowships the historians exceed even the English scholars in their greed, though only by $1,000. Political science, economics, geography, psychology, sociology and anthropology follow in that order. The final set of figures, which cover research grants, will be the most surprising, at least to those who believe that a sharp pencil is sophisticated technology for historians, while their cousins in the social sciences expend millions on computers, anthropological digs, and aerial photography. The psychologists stand at the head of the list, but the historians are a very close second, each discipline having received more than $500,000. Sociology, economics, political science, anthropology and geography complete the field. The point of these obviously limited figures is not to fan the flames of interdisciplinary jealousies. It is merely to suggest that in the field of social science the historians probably write more books and articles and absorb more research funds than scholars in any other discipline.

That observation is merely meant as a prelude to the more difficult, and important, question of quality. At this point the last pretence of value-free analysis will be cast to the winds. My assessment of the quality of the work being done must obviously be personal, though I hope not idiosyncratic. It will also be limited to Canadian studies for reasons of space and competence. Yet a word must be said about historians in non-Canadian areas, for these are very often the people who have moved more quickly than historians of Canada into the use of current social science methods. The work of George Rudé and that of John Bosher are well known among European social historians. The same can be said of John Norris and John Beattie in English history. To this totally arbitrary list should be added the names of John Flint, Gabriel Kolko and Michael Katz. Many of these scholars are not Canadians by birth, but their presence in Canadian universities has helped to broaden our intellectual horizons. They are, after all, working with students who will ultimately adapt their approaches to the needs of Canadian studies. To those who view this development as a threat to the national integrity of Canadian studies,[15] the reply must be that 'foreign' influences apparently were not debilitating in the cases of Léon Gérin, Michel Brunet, Harold Innis or C.B. Macpherson.

In assessing the state of Canadian historical studies nearly seven years ago, I expressed the opinion that Canadian historians had overemphasized so-called national questions. Nationalism and the quest for the elusive Canadian national identity seemed to me to have often blinded our historians, English- and French-speaking, to some of the more fundamental realities of Canadian life: regional, ethnic, and class distinctions. *La nouvelle vague* for Canadian historians – though it was hardly new in other countries – appeared to me to flow in the direction of local history, and historical studies that would probe the depths of the social, professional, economic and intellectual foundations of Canadian society, instead of reworking the endless clichés about Canada's search for survival.[16]

That message was hardly original. Others preached it earlier and more eloquently,[17] and some even practised what they preached. Indeed the thesis may even have been more a reflection of the times than a manifesto; since 1967, much Canadian historical writing has turned in the hoped-for direction and with the aid of the other social sciences new ways of looking at Canadian society have begun to take shape.

Whether they are better ways only the future will tell, for they are still in an early stage of development. At this juncture only a progress report can be presented.

Let me begin by saying that there are many ways of doing history and that in emphasizing the socio-cultural approach, it is not necessary to downgrade biography or political and constitutional history, areas in which Canadian historians have previously distinguished themsleves. Those fields remain available for further exploitation. For example, half a dozen good professional biographies of Canadian businessmen would add a major dimension to our understanding of the past. Anyone can name his candidates: Sir William Van Horn, Sir Rodolphe Forget, Sir Herbert Holt, Sir Donald Mann, Alfred Dubuc, Chester Massey, Isaac Walton Killam. So, too, there is still much to be learned about the Canadian political system. Indeed, apart from Jack Granatstein's fine study of the Conservative party during World War II,[18] the major Canadian parties have hardly been examined. On the other hand we might benefit from a moratorium on CCF and Social-Credit studies, though works like those of Walter Young on the Socialist party,[19] and Maurice Pinard on the Quebec Social-Credit movement[20] provide models worth testing in other contexts. Future biographical work might well benefit from the growing social-science literature pointing toward psycho-history, following the example of Louis Chevrette's recent study of the ultramontains in late-nineteenth-century Quebec.[21] Robert Coles has recently reminded us that the pitfalls of this approach are enormous, especially for those whose knowledge of psychoanalysis exceeds their knowledge of history.[22] But with subjects like Louis Riel, William Aberhart and, above all, Mackenzie King waiting on the couch, the need for a psycho-historian is obvious. So too, politico-constitutional studies can be given new life by placing them more firmly in a socio-economic context.[23]

A recent and still unpublished study of the relations between the federal government and the province of Ontario suggests the potential value of this approach. Christopher Armstrong's study of the 1896-1940 period goes well beyond the usual, somewhat abstract, questions of 'provincial rights', federal disallowance powers and so on, to analyse the fashion in which economic interest groups have utilized one level of government or the other, as the occasion demanded, to achieve explicit economic goals.[24] This type of study was made possible, in part, by an earlier historical study guided by a political economy approach. This was H.V. Nelles's 'Politics of Development', a detailed examination of Ontario resource exploitation policy.[25] These two studies of Ontario suggest an approach that could usefully be applied elsewhere. It would be interesting, for example, to look at the way in which vested economic interests in Quebec have been able to maximize the rhetoric of nationalism in federal-provincial relations.

There are other examples of the potential that a reunion of politics and economics may hold. No book in the last decade has made such an impact or created more controversy than did Fernand Ouellet's massive and brilliant *Histoire économique et sociale du Québec, 1760-1850.*[26] In that volume Ouellet has attempted, with great success, to relate economic fluctuations to social transformation and political upheaval. To do so he has called to his aid statistical material, social theory and an acute understanding of ideological development. Naturally a book covering so extensive a period, and filled with such vexed historical questions as the British Conquest, the beginnings of French-Canadian nationalism, and the Rebellion of 1837, was bound to produce strong reactions. Some have been rather polemical.[27] But more significant is the cooperative work of Gilles Paquet, an economist, and Jean Pierre Wallot, a historian, who together have attempted to bring the whole elaborate theory of systems analysis and the 'new economic history' into battle against Ouellet. While the war is far from over, it has begun to produce from both camps much useful new information which will help to reinterpret nineteenth-century Quebec.[28]

A sound grasp of economics also informs two other significant studies of Quebec history. Jean Hamelin and Yves Roby carry Ouellet's story to the end of the nineteenth century, though in a rather less challenging way, perhaps because their period is less controversial.[29] W.F. Ryan's *The Clergy and Economic Growth, 1896-1914* skilfully draws together economic and cultural history in order to offer an important interpretation of the role played by French Canadians in the industrialization of Quebec.[30]

A somewhat more innovative approach to Canadian historical development is the work of Peter George, who has sought to bring the methodology of cost-benefit analysis to bear upon our national dream, the Canadian Pacific Railway. Following the path of some of the new economic historians in the United States, he has argued that the railway's economic benefits have been overestimated, and that the CPR could have been built with less generous government assistance.[31] The argument, it must be admitted, did not make much impact on Pierre Berton. But then neither did Harold Innis's study of some fifty years earlier![32] Another interesting re-examination by an economist of an old historical problem is John Allen's attempt to build a model of economic interest in voting and to apply it to the election of 1911 on the issue of reciprocity. From his study Allen concludes that economic self-interest alone could explain the result of that contest, obviating recourse to such heady questions as nationalism, imperialism and continentalism.[33] This approach is extremely interesting, and useful, especially when it brings the historian down from the clouds of rhetoric to the solid ground of measurable fact. But there is, nevertheless, a danger in this type of history, for it can force an untidy past into an abstract model or ignore those features which do not fit the model. It may well be that the CPR could have been built on terms more fair to the Canadian taxpayer. But that conclusion really only sharpens the focus of the question the historian must still answer: why was it built on the terms that it was? Here Pierre Berton may be nearer the heart of the matter than the practioners of cost-benefit analysis.

Some of the techniques of the new economic historians are also being brought into play by urban historians. This is an area of enormous promise, and one which historians of Canada are just beginning to open up. Here there are at least two trends in evidence. F.H. Armstrong and Alan Artibise have approached the histories of Toronto and Winnipeg respectively over a broad sweep, attempting to pull together many facets of a city's life.[34] Some similar work has been launched in Quebec by Paul-André Linteau, among others.[35] This is a very valid approach, even when it produces as traditional a book as J.I. Cooper's splendid little study of Montreal.[36] Another approach has been adopted by Michael Katz, in his exhaustive examination of Hamilton, and by the geographer Peter Goheen in his seminal study, *Victorian Toronto, 1850 to 1900.*[37] Both of these researchers have made use of large quantities of local government statistics while attempting to look at the social configuration in a way which reveals something of the lives of the people who normally do not get into the history books. Katz's interest is in questions of social structure and social mobility, and if he succeeds in putting almost every mid-Victorian Hamiltonian through the computer, we will know more, and perhaps more of significance, about Hamilton than about any other North-American city.[38] Professor Goheen's imaginative study is concerned with the broad question of urban transformation, of the rise of the 'new city'. While his book is often highly technical in its discussion of methodology, there can be no question that he has established an exceptionally revealing approach to urban historical studies. Katz and Goheen, with their new methodologies, have important things to teach us. But as Paul Rutherford's excellent essay on urban reform in the early decades of the twentieth century illustrates, there is still much that can be learned through a closer examination of traditional sources.[39]

The study of urban history leads naturally to questions of social classes and industrial development. One method of focusing on this problem is to examine the labouring classes. This is still a largely untouched field, though the body of literature dealing with trade-union history is growing. The work of Stuart Jamieson, Irving Abella and Paul Phillips, among others, is gradually closing an important gap in our history. Perhaps more interesting, and suggestive of the direction in which historians of the working class should move, is the still unpublished work of David Bercusson, Donald Avery and Terry Copp. Bercusson's study of labour in Winnipeg during World War I has placed the Winnipeg Strike in a whole new context, allowing us to see working conditions, inter-union disputes, and a changing political climate, all of which make the 1919 explosion much more understandable. Avery's examination of immigration policy and the 'foreign navvy' offers many new insights into class and ethnic attitudes during the Laurier years. Finally, Terry Copp's study of the condition of the working class in early twentieth-century Montreal promises to be a major work of Canadian social history.[40] The shift from trade-union history to working-class history is a development of major significance comparable to a shift from political to social history. That shift is evident in both English- and French-Canadian writing,[41] and should contribute enormously to a fuller understanding of Canadian society. It is useful, however, to be reminded from time to time that not everything is new. One of the first and still one of the best studies of working-class life in Canada was published forty-five years ago. The recent reissue of Edwin Bradwin's *Bunkhouse Man*, taken together with Rex Lucas's *Minetown, Milltown, Railtown*, displays what historians can learn from the observational techniques and the analysis of sociologists.[42]

Concern about class and social structure can also be seen in some of the new work in the field of educational history. Some historians, such as Susan Houston, have begun to analyse educational institutions and ideologies in relation to social change and social control.[43] Robert Stamp's study of technical education, and Douglas Lawr's work on agricultural education, have transformed the sometimes arid field of education history into extremely revealing social studies.[44] There is work of a similar kind taking place in Quebec, though there, as is often the case, the relationship among education, the Church and nationalism gives much of that work a special flavour. It can be sampled in an excellent collection of interdisciplinary essays entitled *Ecole et société au Québec*, edited by Pierre Bélanger and Guy Rocher.[45]

While there often seems to be a conflict between the practitioners of social history and those whose interest lies in intellectual history, that old idealist-materialist conflict is really rather academic. The study of intellectual history can easily be meshed with social history, as exemplified by the work of Carl Berger, Richard Allen, and George Emery. Allen's work on the social gospel is an obvious case in point: the men and ideas he analyses can be understood only if they are placed against the socio-economic background of a society moving into an increasingly industrial-urban setting. The same can be said of Joseph Levitt's study of the nationalist movement in Quebec at the beginning of this century.[47] Stewart and Rawlyk's study of religion and society in late eighteenth-century Nova Scotia,[48] and the excellent collection of essays on the role of the layman in the Quebec church recently published by a group of young Quebec historians,[49] again illustrate Lucien Febvre's contention that there is no such thing as social, political, religious or economic history: 'There is just history.'[50]

The study of social movements is yet another area where the various approaches to history flow together and where some social science methodology can usefully be applied. Prohibition,[51] which until recently has been largely ignored by Canadian historians, is one example. Here is a successful reform movement. That in itself makes it rather unusual in Canadian history. To explain the success, a study of ideology and organization will provide only partial answers. Some recent work, still unpublished for the most part, suggests that the movement for prohibition has to be seen partly in terms of class, partly in terms of ethnicity, and certainly in relation to a rapidly changing society. The woman suffrage movement, another successful demand for reform, also needs to be examined in some such terms as these. Thorough studies of the role of women in Canadian history are still few in number, but there are some signs that contemporary controversies will help to encourage research in this important and interesting area.[52]

Before concluding this catalogue of Canadiana there is one more highly significant area that deserves comment. This is the study of ethnic history. The term is a somewhat unfortunate one, but there seems to be no entirely satisfactory substitute. In any event it is history that is concerned with immigration, settlement and the whole question of assimilation and cultural pluralism. It is not a new area of work: the sociologist C.A. Dawson long ago showed us the way;[53] but there is a revived interest in the subject, perhaps related to the discussion of the 'national question' in Canada in recent years. Some very good work has begun to appear. Five years ago George Woodcock and Ivan Avakumovic published a book on the Doukhobors, which can hardly be too highly praised. The subject is difficult and controversial, but those two writers examined it with the kind of skill and objectivity which only the best historians ever achieve. Victor Peters, a sociologist, adopted a different approach to his subject, the Hutterian brethren, but his little book is also a valuable contribution to our history. Of many other volumes in this area three, at least, deserve mention. V.J. Kaye's *Early Ukrainian Settlements in Canada* and J.G. MacGregor's somewhat more popular *Vilni Zemli*, which is a history of Ukrainian settlement in northern Alberta, both indicate what a rich vein ethnic history can be. John Norris's broad study of ethnic groups in British Columbia points towards a synthesis and offers some suggestive comments on patterns of pluralism and assimilation.[54]

One dimension of ethnic history which is likely to result in some substantial revisions of at least a few of the most cherished myths of

Canadian society is the question of ethnic tolerance. It is often assumed that Canadians planned their nation as a mosaic, distinct from the melting pot in the United States.[55] Recent studies leave little of this contention intact. Most English Canadians preferred the melting pot pattern, and often wanted to throw French Canadians into the pot with all the recent immigrants. The outcome was most often intended to be what an American sociologist has called 'anglo-conformity'.[56] French Canadians, too, favoured such an outcome, though seeking to preserve the two 'charter' groups. John Porter's *Vertical Mosaic* has been suggestive to historians, and some have begun to look into past ethnic relations. The results are not yet complete, but existing studies strongly suggest that if the concept of the mosaic is a Canadian virtue, it became one out of necessity.[57]

It would be gratifying to be able to report that interest in ethnic studies has been paralleled by similar developments in the history of the native people of Canada. Unfortunately that does not seem to be possible. Here is an area, of course, where historians need much assistance from other social scientists. Bruce Trigger's study of the Hurons[58] indicates that in the present, as in the past, the anthropologists are far better equipped than the historians to develop this aspect of Canadian studies. Peter Usher's controversial report on the Banks-landers, the so-called Hawthorn report, and an especially stimulating essay by Henry Zentner suggest the same conclusion.[59] A study of Canadian historical writing designed to reveal the fashion in which the native peoples have been treated provides dismal, even shameful, results.[60]

Perhaps things are changing. Certainly there is evidence of serious interest among today's students in the history of native peoples, and one recent volume which should further stimulate this interest is Morris Zaslow's *The Opening of the Canadian North, 1870-1914.*[61] This book typifies in several ways some of the recent trends in Canadian historical writing by making effective use of findings of other social-science scholars. It is difficult to praise this book too highly: the scholarship is meticulous, the writing clear, and the attempt to comprehend a total society over an extended period is both commendable and convincing. It is the history of a society, and that is what Canadian history should now be attempting. Professor Zaslow's book is an excellent example of the way in which a historian can master a broad range of social science information and incorporate it into his work, while all the time remaining a historian.

This assessment of the work of historians in Canada is obviously an optimistic one. That optimism seems justified, since much fine work has been done in the past decade, though some remains as yet unpublished. Taken together this work already suggests important ways in which our understanding of the Canadian past must be reshaped. But that optimism is also based on a conviction that historical studies in Canada are moving in rewarding directions. These directions are towards further concentrated study of social structure and social change through time. That can best be done by continuing to work with such concepts as regionalism, ethnicity and class. There are, of course, new areas that need investigation. Demography, for example, has been largely ignored by English-Canadian historians, though French Canadians have done some important work.[62] Vivian Nelles has recently suggested in a brilliant essay that there is much to be learned from historical studies of the professions in Canada,[63] and the analysis of family history has been cogently urged by others.[64] Studies of bureaucracy, as the recent examination of the history of the Civil Service Commission suggests,[65] should help us to understand much about the structure and organization of Canadian society. Finally, the surface of the economic history of modern Canada has barely been scratched, and until that task is taken up systematically it will be impossible to write a convincing new synthesis of our past.

None of these assignments can be taken on by historians alone, for they demand the skills and methodologies of all the social sciences. Skills and methodologies are, of course, no substitute for the historian's most necessary quality – creative judgment. But that creative judgment can be set free on new paths through the disciplined use of social-science insights, hypotheses and techniques. In short, my gratuitous advice to fellow historians is: break the decalogue, commit a social science. That way we can approximate, at least, the goal of the historian as defined by J.H. Plumb. The historian's aim, he writes, 'is to understand men both as individuals and in their social relationships in time. Social embraces all man's activities – economic, religious, political, artistic, legal, military, scientific – everything, indeed, that affects the life of mankind. And this, of course, is not a static study but a study of movement and change.'[66]

The discipline of history, invertebrate or marsupial, need have no fear of the other social sciences, provided it is prepared to learn from them.

NOTES

1 J.H. Hexter, 'The Rhetoric of History,' *International Encyclopedia of Social Sciences,* VI (New York, 1968), p.370

2 E.H. Carr, *What is History?* (Random House, 1961), p.111

3 G.R. Elton, *The Practice of History* (Methuen, 1967), p.12

4 On this subject see H. Stuart Hughes, 'The Historian and the Social Scientist,' *American Historical Review,* LXVI (October 1960), pp.20-46; and J.H. Hexter, *The History Primer* (Basic Books, 1971), pp.86 ff.

5 William H. Dray, 'Theories of Historical Understanding,' *Transactions of the Royal Society of Canada,* fourth series, VIII (1970), pp.267-86

6 Hexter, 'The Rhetoric of History,' p.380

7 William O. Aydelotte, *Quantification in History* (Addison-Wesley, 1971), p.36

8 Stephan Thernstrom, 'Reflections on the New Urban History,' *Daedalus,* C (Spring 1971), p.371

9 I have borrowed this phrase from H. Stuart Hughes who uses it in an opposite sense, as a weakness rather than a strength. See his *History as Art and Science* (Harper and Row, 1964), p.1

10 D.G. Creighton, *Harold Adams Innis: Portrait of a Scholar* (Toronto, 1957); and Robin Neill, *A New Theory of Value: The Canadian Economics of H.A. Innis* (Toronto, 1972)

11 Public Archives of Canada, *Register of Post-Graduate Dissertations in Progress in History and Related Subjects* (Canadian Historical Association, no 1, 1966 and no 7, 1972)

12 Carl Berger, 'History Studies in English,' in *Supplement to The Oxford Companion to Canadian History and Literature,* William Toye, gen. ed. (Oxford, 1973)

13 David P. Gagan, *Prairie Perspectives* (Holt, Rinehart and Winston, 1970); and Henry C. Klassen and Anthony W. Rasporich, *Prairie Perspectives,* 2 (Holt, Rinehart and Winston, 1973)

14 *The Canada Council, 15th Annual Report, 1971-1972* (Information Canada, 1972), pp.62-8

15 Michael Butler and David Shugarman, 'Americanization and Scholarly Values,' *Journal of Canadian Studies,* V (August 1970), pp.12-27; and Michael Gurstein, 'Towards the Nationalization of Canadian Sociology,' *Journal of Canadian Studies,* VII (1972), pp.50-8

16 Ramsay Cook, 'Canadian Historical Writing,' *Scholarship in Canada, 1967,*
   R.H. Hubbard, ed. (Toronto, 1968), pp.79-81
17 J.M.S. Careless, ' "Limited Identities" in Canada,' *Canadian Historical Review,*
   L (March 1969), pp.1-10
18 J.L. Granatstein, *The Politics of Survival* (Toronto, 1967)
19 Walter D. Young, *The Anatomy of a Party: The National CCF, 1932-61*
   (Toronto, 1969)
20 Maurice Pinard, *The Rise of a Third Party* (Prentice-Hall, 1971); and Michael
   B. Stein, *The Dynamics of Right Wing Protest. A Political Analysis of Social
   Credit in Quebec* (Toronto, 1973)
21 Louis Chevrette, 'Aspets de la psychologie du groupe de pression ultramontain
   canadien-français (1870-1890),' *Revue d'histoire de l'Amérique française,*
   XXV (September 1972), pp.155-90
22 Robert Coles, 'Shrinking History,' *New York Review of Books,* 22 February
   1973, pp.15-21 and 8 March 1973, pp.25-9
23 Jacques le Goff, 'Is Politics Still the Backbone of History?,' *Daedalus,* C
   (Winter 1971), pp.1-19
24 Christopher Armstrong, 'The Politics of Federalism: Ontario's Relations with
   the Federal Government 1896-1941,' unpublished PhD dissertation, University
   of Toronto, 1972
25 H.V. Nelles, 'The Politics of Development: Forests, Mines and Hydro-Electric
   Development in Ontario, 1890-1939' unpublished PhD dissertation, University
   of Toronto, 1970
26 Fernand Ouellet, *Histoire économique et sociale du Québec, 1760-1850*
   (Editions Fides, 1966)
27 Michel Brunet, *Les Canadiens après la Conquête, 1759-1775* (Editions Fides,
   1969); and Maurice Séguin, *La Nation canadienne et l'agriculture (1760-1850)*
   (Editions le Boréal Express, 1970)
28 Gilles Paquet and Jean-Pierre Wallot, 'Canada 1760-1850: anamorphose et
   prospectives,' *Economie québecoise,* Robert Comeau *et al.,* eds. (Université du
   Québec, 1969), pp.255-300; 'Crise agricole et tensions socioethniques dans le
   bas Canada, 1802-1812: eléments pour une ré-interpretation,' *Revue d'histoire
   de l'Amérique française,* XXVI (September 1972), pp.185-238; 'International
   Circumstances of Lower Canada, 1786-1910: Prolegomenon,' *Canadian
   Historical Review,* LIII (December 1972), pp.371-401; and Fernand Ouellet,
   Eléments d'histoire sociale du Bas-Canada (Editions HMH, 1972)
29 Jean Hamelin and Yves Roby, *Histoire économique du Québec, 1851-1896*
   (Editions Fides, 1972); see also Albert Faucher, *Histoire économiqe et
   unité canadienne* (Editions Fides, 1970); and Louis Dechême, 'Les
   Entreprises de William Price," *'Histoire sociale/Social History,* I
   (April 1968), pp.16-52
30 W.F. Ryan, *The Clergy and Economic Growth in Quebec, 1896-1914* (Laval,
   1966)

31 Peter George, 'Recent Developments in the Quantification of Canadian Economic History,' *Histoire sociale/Social History*, IV (1969), and his introduction to H.A. Innis, *A History of the Canadian Pacific Railway*, second ed. (Toronto, 1970)

32 See H.V. Nelles, 'The Ties that Bind: Berton's CPR,' *The Canadian Forum*, L (November-December 1970), pp.270-2

33 John Allan, 'Reciprocity and the Canadian General Election of 1911: A Re-Examination of Economic Self-Interest in Voting,' unpublished master's thesis, Queen's University, 1971

34 F.H. Armstrong, 'Toronto in Transition, 1828-38,' unpublished PhD dissertation, University of Toronto, 1965); and Alan Artibise, 'The Urban Development of Winnipeg, 1874-1914' unpublished PhD dissertation, University of British Columbia, 1972

35 Paul-André Linteau, 'L'Histoire urbaine au Québec: bilan et tendences,' *Urban History Review*, I (February 1972), pp.7-10

36 J.I. Cooper, *Montreal: A Brief History* (McGill-Queen's, 1969)

37 Peter G. Goheen, *Victorian Toronto, 1850 to 1900* (Chicago, Department of Geography, 1970)

38 Michael Katz, 'Social Structure in Hamilton, Ontario,' *Nineteenth Century Cities: Essays in the New Urban History*, Stephan Thernstrom and Richard Sennett, eds. (Yale, 1969), pp.209-24; and 'The People of a Canadian City, 1851-2,' *Canadian Historical Review*, LIII (December 1972), 402-25

39 Paul Rutherford, 'Tomorrow's Metropolis: The Urban Reform Movement in Canada, 1880-1920,' *Canadian Historical Association Historical Papers, 1971* (Canadian Historical Association, 1971), pp.203-24

40 Stuart Jamieson, *Times of Trouble: Labour Unrest and Industrial Conflict in Canada, 1900-66* (Ottawa, Privy Council Office, 1968); Irving Abella, *Nationalism, Communism and Canadian Labour* (Toronto, 1973); Paul Phillips, *No Power Greater* (Vancouver, Federation of Labour and Boag Foundation, 1967); David J. Bercusson, 'Labour in Winnipeg: The Great War and the General Strike,' unpublished PhD dissertation, University of Toronto, 1971; Donald Avery, 'Canadian Immigration Policy and the Foreign Navvy, 1896-1914,' (mimeographed); and T.J. Copp, 'The Condition of the Working Class in Montreal, 1897-1920,' (mimeographed)

41 Hélène Espessat, Jean-Pierre Hardy and Thierry Ruddell, 'Le Monde du Travail au Québec au XVIIe et au XIXe siècles,' *Revue d'histoire de l'Amérique française*, 25 (March 1972), pp.499-539

42 Edmund Bradwin, *The Bunkhouse Man*, second ed. (Toronto, 1972); Rex A. Lucas, *Minetown, Milltown, Railtown* (Toronto, 1971)

43 Susan E. Houston, 'Politics, Schools and Social Change in Upper Canada,' *Canadian Historical Review*, LIII (September 1972), pp.249-71; 'Education and Social Change in English-Speaking Canada,' *History of Education Quarterly*, special issue, XII (Fall 1972)

44 Robert M. Stamp, 'The Campaign for Technical Education in Ontario, 1876-1914,' unpublished PhD dissertation, University of Western Ontario, 1970; and Douglas A. Lawr, 'The Development of Agricultural Education in Ontario,' unpublished PhD dissertation, University of Toronto, 1969

45 Pierre Bélanger and Guy Rocher, eds., *Ecole et société au Québec* (Editions HMH, 1970)

46 Carl Berger, *The Sense of Power* (Toronto, 1970); Richard Allen, *The Social Passion* (Toronto, 1972); and George Emery, 'Methodism on the Canadian Prairies, 1896-1914,' unpublished PhD dissertation, University of British Columbia, 1970

47 Joseph Levitt, *Henri Bourassa and the Golden Calf* (Les Editions de l'Université d'Ottawa, 1969)

48 Gordon Stewart and George Rawlyk, *A People Highly Favoured of God* (Macmillan, 1972)

49 Pierre Hurtubise, *Le Laic dans l'Eglise canadienne-française de 1830 à nos jours* (Editions Fides, 1972)

50 Lucien Febvre, *Combats pour l'histoire* (Libraire Armand Colin, 1953), p.20

51 John H. Thompson, 'The Prohibition Question in Manitoba, 1892-1928,' unpublished MA thesis, Simon Fraser University, 1969; and Erhart Pinno, 'Temperance and Prohibition in Saskatchewan,' unpublished MA thesis, University of Saskatchewan, Regina, 1969

52 C.L. Cleverdon, *The Woman Suffrage Movement in Canada* (Toronto, 1950); June Menzies, 'Votes for Saskatchewan Women,' *Politics in Saskatchewan*, Norman Ward and Duff Spafford, eds. (Longman, 1968); and Carol Lee Bacchi-Ferraro, 'The Ideas of Canadian Suffragists, 1890-1920,' unpublished MA thesis, McGill University, 1970

53 C.A. Dawson, *Group Settlement: Ethnic Communities in Western Canada* (Macmillan, 1936)

54 George Woodcock and Ivan Avakumovic, *The Doukhobors* (Oxford, 1968); Victor Peters, *All Things Common* (Minnesota, 1965); V.J. Kaye, *Early Ukrainian Settlements in Canada, 1895-1900* (Toronto, 1964); J.G. Mac-Gregor, *Vilni-Zemli* (McClelland and Stewart, 1969); and John Norris, *Strangers Entertained* (British Columbia Centennial '71 Committee, 1971)

55 Allan Smith, 'Metaphor and Nationality in North America,' *Canadian Historical Review*, II (September 1970), pp.247-75

56 Milton M. Gordon, *Assimilation in American Life* (Oxford, 1964)

57 Marilyn Barber, introduction to J.S. Woodsworth, *Strangers within Our Gates* (Toronto, 1972), pp.vi-xxiii; Howard Palmer, 'Responses to Foreign Immigration: Nativism and Ethnic Tolerance in Alberta, 1880-1930,' unpublished MA thesis, University of Alberta, 1970; Morris Mott, 'The Foreign Peril: Nativism in Winnipeg, 1916-22,' unpublished MA thesis, University of Manitoba, 1972; Andrew Milner, 'The New Politics and Ethnic Revolt, 1929-38,' Norman Ward and Duff Spafford, eds., pp.150-77; and Claudette Bégin-Wolff, 'L'opinion

publique québecoise face à l'immigration, (1906-1913),' unpublished MA thesis, Université de Montréal, 1970

58 Bruce Trigger, *The Huron Farmers of the North* (Holt, Rinehart and Winston, 1969)

59 Peter J. Usher, *The Bankslanders: Economy and Ecology of a Frontier Trapping Community*, vol. III, *The Community* (National Library of Canada, 1971); H.B. Hawthorn, ed., *A Survey of the Contemporary Indians of Canada* 2 vols. (Indian Affairs Branch, 1966-7); and Henry Zentner, 'The Impending Identity Crisis among Native Peoples,' David P. Gagan, ed., pp.78-91

60 James W. St G. Walker, 'The Indian in Canadian Historical Writing,' *CHA, Historical Papers, 1971*, pp.21-51

61 Morris Zaslow, *The Opening of the Canadian North, 1870-1914* (McClelland and Stewart, 1971)

62 See for example, Jacques Légaré, Yolande Lavoie and Robert Charbonneau, 'The Early Canadian Population: The Problems in Automatic Record Linkage,' *Canadian Historical Review*, LIII (December 1972), pp.427-42

63 H.V. Nelles, introduction to T.C. Keefer, *The Philosophy of Railroads* (Toronto, 1972), ix-lxiii

64 F.H. Armstrong, 'The Family: Some Aspects of a Neglected Approach to Canadian Historical Studies,' *CHA, Historical Papers, 1971*, pp.112-24; and David Gagan and Herbert Mays, 'Historical Demography and Canadian Social History: Families and Land in Peel County,' *Canadian Historical Review*, LIV (March 1973), pp.27-47

65 J.E. Hodgetts *et al.*, *The Biography of an Institution: The Civil Service Commission of Canada, 1908-1967* (McGill-Queen's, 1972)

66 J.H. Plumb, *The Death of the Past* (Houghton Mifflin, 1970), p.105

Commentary P. DANSEREAU

Professor Cook's statement that 'the good historian ... can never wholly reject his humanistic heritage' leads me to the melancholy thought that this is exactly what several generations of scientists have done, from the mid-nineteenth century to this day. Bertrand Russell has repeatedly denounced this heretical schizophrenia. In my own modest voice I have pleaded with fellow 'scientists' to be present in their work and not to reject the first person singular as though it would ruin their credibility.

A matter of style? Yes. It was precisely a great natural scientist, Buffon, who said: 'Le style c'est l'homme.' And is it not between men that a reconciliation of the 'two cultures' will take place? And must they not all speak with their own voice, paying great attention to how they speak and not trust that what they say will shine through a deficient prose and a halting misuse of language?

Common stakes are also established by historians and natural scientists in their claims for the autonomy of their discipline. The need to borrow from far afield and the development of strictly disciplinary concepts and methodology are always in conflict. The days when history was strictly historical are far behind us. It is heartening to witness how well some historians have assimilated the findings of economics, anthropology, and sociology, but possibly disturbing to watch some historians throw themselves wholly into the orbit of sociology. Surely history, as a discipline, has a hard enough core to maintain its attraction for the mind of scholars and for the preoccupations of society.

Among the influences which I would personally welcome in the writing of history is a greater influx of spatial references. Some historians have been very poor geographers, to the extent that the landscapes within which they have recorded their dramas have been in such soft focus that they did not truly relate to the action that was being depicted. It is hardly necessary to be a determinist in order to acknowledge the pressures of environment by specifying its elements in a recognizable way.

This would almost lead me to a plea that historians become ecologists. Quite seriously, I do believe that something of the kind will happen. I was taught history, as a child, in terms of great battles won and lost. Military heroics gave place to political speculation (for example, on the origins of the Frech revolution) and to economic debunking (for example, of the Crusades), not to mention the sociological everyday-life approach and the eventual onset of psychoanalysis on a large scale. Each of these turnovers favoured the developing disciplines, each of which was freeing itself from earlier compasses, among them history itself.

It therefore seems not improbable to rewrite history in post-Keynesian, post-Stalinian, post-Orwellian terms as the story of man's escalating power over environment, where each chapter concerns itself with resource exploitation and landscape management by fluctuating populations. The emphasis could well be displaced from the military or cultural dominance to the varieties of ways in which circuits of exchange are operated in the course of resource sharing.

Finally, I feel that a study of history is the only way in which an individual can steep a feeling of continuity which is so essential to social participation. In these days of flagging motivation, no discipline offers better opportunities of discovering our personal and collective affinities. No one who is pleased to live in the present can wholly nourish his spirit with contemporary heroes and villains, thinkers and doers, artists and scientists. Some of our closest of kin died long before we were born. Do we want them to speak to us?

M. ROKEACH

5
Some reflections about the place
of values in Canadian social science

On this happy occasion of the Official Opening of the Social Science
Centre at the University of Western Ontario it is ceremoniously fitting
and intellectually proper to offer some reflections – if you will,
visions – about the role that the new Centre might play in the life of
this university and in the life of the larger Canadian society of which it
is a part.* The fact that your new home has been officially identified as
the Social Science Centre rather than, more perfunctorily, say, the
Social Science Building points at the very least to the hopes and aspirations of those who were responsible for its realization. Dean G.L.
Reuber's invitational letter was a call for a conference that would
provide an occasion for stock taking and more specifically, for observations and suggestions about the role that the new Centre might play in
improving the quality of undergraduate and graduate instruction, in
fostering interdisciplinary associations, and stimulating research within
our respective disciplines, especially research that would be appropriate
in a distinctively Canadian context.

My reflections derive from a certain kind of perspective that I think
should be made explicit. First, I spent two stimulating and productive
years as a visiting professor of psychology at the University of Western
Ontario (1970-2). During this time I taught undergraduate and graduate

* Certain portions of this paper are adapted from my recently published *The
Nature of Human Values.*

courses in social psychology, and I had occasion to meet and interact with students and also with colleagues from various disciplines, particularly in psychology, sociology, anthropology, geography, and political science. Second, my perspective is that of a social psychologist whose main research preoccupation in recent years has been with the problem of values: what they are, how they are measured, how they are organized into systems of values, their employment as social indicators of quality of life, their cultural and institutional origins, their attitudinal and behavioural consequences, and the conditions under which they might undergo change.

Given such a theoretical perspective, it is perhaps inevitable that I would seek to formulate the role of the new Social Science Centre as a question of values. Every social institution within a society may be conceptualized as specializing in the maintenance and enhancement of certain subsets of values, and in their transmission from generation to generation. Thus, the religious institutions of society specialize in maintaining, enhancing, and transmitting certain values that we call religious values; the family is an institution that specializes in another subset of values; academic, political, economic, and legal institutions specialize in yet other subsets of values. I therefore believe that it might be appropriate on this special occasion to ask several questions. First, exactly which values should the Social Science Centre attempt to specialize in, to foster, maintain, enhance, and transmit, in its training of undergraduate and graduate students, in its encouragement of interdisciplinary associations, and in its pursuit of new knowledge? Second, what special problems can this particular Social Science Centre be expected to encounter, in this particular university and in this particular country, in achieving its aim of advancing and enhancing these values? And, third, how can the Social Science Centre best organize or arrange itself in order to implement its goal of furthering the attainment of these values?

In addressing myself to such difficult questions of values I believe that it would be especially pertinent if I were first to try to bring together whatever data there may already be available on the values of the three main constituents of any university – faculty, graduate students and undergraduate students. These data come from a variety of sources in the United States, Canada and other countries; when brought together from all these diverse sources they inform us about the values of faculty members, including those in social science, about graduate student values, and about undergraduate student values in several countries, including Canadian undergraduates tested at the University of Western Ontario. These data, although not altogether representative of their respective populations, are nonetheless sufficiently representative, and are, moreover, sufficiently dissonance-producing to serve as a useful point of departure for examining the role that this Social Science Centre might play in improving the quality of life of its undergraduate and graduate students, its faculty, and also, hopefully, the quality of life of the larger society of which it is an integral part.

The empirical data included here, concerning the values of faculty, graduate, and undergraduate students, are at least comparable in the sense that they were all obtained with the same psychometric instrument, the Rokeach Value Survey (1967). This instrument was designed to provide a simple and economical measure of human values and value systems. It consists of one alphabetically arranged list of eighteen values which I call *terminal* values because they refer to 'end-states of existence', and another alphabetically arranged list of eighteen values which I call *instrumental* values because they refer to 'modes of behaviour', these modes of behaviour being instrumental to the attainment of the terminal end-states of existence. Respondents are requested to rank each set of alphabetically arranged values in the order of their importance 'as guiding principles in your daily life'. These terminal and instrumental values, along with their defining phrases, are shown in Tables 1 and 2. They were selected after extensive research which was designed to produce a reasonably comprehensive and universal list of human values, and for this reason I am inclined to believe that the Value Survey provides us with meaningful cross-cultural value comparisons.

To date, the Rokeach Value Survey has been successfully employed in many research projects with respondents ranging in age from eleven to ninety years (Rokeach 1973) and from all social classes (Rokeach and Parker 1971). The average adult requires about fifteen to twenty minutes to complete the rankings. As with any measuring instrument, there is the question of its reliability and validity. With time intervals of two to four months, the test-retest reliabilities of the terminal and instrumental value rankings are 0.76 and 0.65, respectively; with longer time intervals of fourteen to sixteen months, the test-retest reliabilities of the terminal and instrumental value rankings are still reasonably good – 0.69 and 0.61, respectively. As for validity, approximately one-third of the thirty-six values in the Value Survey have been found to be statistically significant indicators of various kinds of social attitudes (for example, towards religion, race, politics), and also of various kinds of behaviours (for example, going to church, duration of eye contacts with blacks, cheating on examinations). Distinctive value patterns have already been found for many different kinds of occupations, life styles, and religious and political groups. For instance, distinctive value patterns have already been found for policemen, entrepreneurs and salesmen, priests, prison inmates, hippies, the rich and the poor, the activist supporters of George Wallace, Richard Nixon, and Hubert Humphrey (Rokeach, Miller and Snyder 1971; Hague 1968; Cochrane 1971; Bishop, Barclay, and Rokeach 1972; Rokeach 1973).

FACULTY VALUES

Tables 1 and 2 show the terminal and instrumental median value rankings for college professors in five academic fields. Next to these medians, in parentheses, are shown the composite value rankings from 1 to 18, that is, the highest median has a composite ranking of 1, the next highest median has a composite ranking of 2, and so on. These professors were tested at Michigan State University and Wayne State University in 1969. Also shown in Tables 1 and 2, for comparative purposes, are the value rankings that were obtained for a national area probability sample of adult Americans over twenty-one who were tested in 1968. A total of 212 faculty members with the rank of assistant professor or higher filled out the Value Survey, and they were selected from the following fields: biological sciences (biology, botany, biochemistry), physical sciences (physics, chemistry, geology), and social sciences (psychology, sociology, political science, anthropology, economics), the arts (music, drama, painting), and business. While it cannot be claimed that this academic sample is an altogether representative one, there is no particularly good reason to suppose that the data thus obtained are unrepresentative. In any event, I believe that these are the only quantitative data available concerning the values of college professors, and they provide us with at least an approximate benchmark of what academic values must be like everywhere.

Nonparametric median tests (Siegel 1956) reveal that only six of the thirty-six values do not differentiate in a statistically significant way the values of academicians from those of nonacademicians. The remaining thirty values do differentiate significantly between them,* and these vary in magnitude, as can be determined by a visual inspection of the data.

Considering first the terminal value findings shown in Table 1, the largest differences between adult Americans and college professors are as follows: while the composite rank of *a sense of accomplishment* is tenth for adult Americans, it is first to third for college professors. Adult Americans rank *an exciting life* last while college professors rank it far more important – anywhere from seventh to fourteenth. Adult Americans rank *salvation* eighth on the average while college professors rank it least important – eighteenth. Adult Americans rank *a comfortable life* ninth while college professors rank it much less important – thirteenth to sixteenth.

Considering next the instrumental value findings shown in Table 2, it will be noticed that the largest difference is obtained for *clean:* adult Americans rank it eighth while academicians rank it seventeenth or eighteenth. This rather large difference cannot be interpreted to mean that college professors are a dirty lot when compared with average Americans. Rather, this difference, along with the rather large difference obtained for rankings of *a comfortable life*, must be attributed to socio-economic differences in values, since other analyses reveal that rankings of *clean* and *a comfortable life* are the two values that best differentiate the poor from the rich, and the uneducated from the educated (Rokeach and Parker 1970).

Yet other differences in instrumental values do seem to reflect differences between academics and nonacademics. Notice that professors

---

* That 30 of the 36 values show statistically significant differences is not surprising, in view of the large number of cases in the national sample (Bakan, 1966). In the final analysis, we are more interested in the magnitude than in the statistical significance of value differences.

rank *intellectual* anywhere from first to fourth, *logical* anywhere from fifth to eighth, and *imaginative* anywhere from third to tenth. In sharp contrast, these same three values are ranked virtually at the bottom of the instrumental value hierarchy by adult Americans. These rather large differences, when considered alongside the rather large differences found for the terminal values *a sense of accomplishment* and *an exciting life*, can perhaps best be summarized by saying that college professors place considerably more value on self-realization and intellectual competence than do adult Americans in general. Conversely, adult Americans care considerably more for the more traditional values of God, home and country, as is evidenced by the greater importance that they place on *salvation, family security*, and *national security.*

There are several other findings that deserve special mention if we are to understand better the values of academia: 1/ The average college professor, who is of course white, ranks *equality* anywhere from third to eighth in importance. The average adult black American ranks *equality* second, and the average adult white American ranks *equality* much lower – eleventh in importance.* This means that white college professors are on the whole considerably more liberal and less racist than the average adult white American. Differences in *equality* rankings have been found to be the best single indicator and predictor of a liberal political outlook (Rokeach 1973). Thus, George Wallace activists in the United States ranked *equality* last on their terminal value hierarchy on the average, Nixon activists ranked *equality* ninth, while Humphrey activists ranked *equality* second (Bishop, Barclay and Rokeach 1972).

2/ Contrary to popular conception, world peace seems to be less salient for college professors than for the average man in the street. The composite rank of *a world at peace* is anywhere from sixth to ninth for college professors, while it is ranked first on the average by adult Americans. Similarly *national security* is ranked twelfth by adult Americans but fifteenth to seventeenth by college professors. These findings may lead us to wonder about the reasons for the greater

---

* Table 1 shows that for the adult American sample the composite ranking of *equality* is seventh. The total sample of adult Americans consisted of about 1,200 whites and 200 blacks, the former ranking *equality* eleventh on the average and the latter ranking it second.

involvement of American college professors in the widespread antiwar protests of the late 1960s. One interpretation is that their greater involvement was not so much a function of their preoccupation with world peace as a function of their belief that the security of their country was not being threatened. The greater involvement of the academic community in the antiwar protest movement can thus be interpreted as being a function of the relatively low salience of these two terminal values, *national security* and *a world at peace*, combined perhaps with the emphasis the movement placed on self-actualization and competence.

3/ As already noted, professors value *an exciting life* far more than do other adult Americans; whereas the average American ranks this value last on their terminal value hierarchy, professors in the various disciplines rank it anywhere from seventh to fourteenth in importance. This difference cannot be interpreted to mean that professors are a hedonistic lot (any more than that they are a dirty lot), since they care for *pleasure* about as little as do other adult Americans. *An exciting life* to college professors evidently means a stimulating, intellectual life.

4/ Adult Americans care considerably more for *happiness* than for inner *harmony*; notice, however, that it is the other way around for college professors.

5/ Similarly, adult Americans care more about being *ambitious* than about being *capable*, which they rank second and ninth respectively; but, again, it is the other way around for college professors, who rank *capable* anywhere from third to sixth and *ambitious* anywhere from sixth to twelfth. To be *ambitious* means to work hard to earn a living, while being *capable* points to a motivation to be effective and competent (White 1959).

6/ Surprisingly, and perhaps even disappointingly, the instrumental value, *courageous*, defined as 'standing up for your beliefs', is somewhat less important to the academic community than to other Americans; whereas it ranks sixth for the American people as a whole, it ranks eighth for college professors. Does this mean that academic tenure, which allegedly evolved in order to encourage intellectual courage has, instead, led to the opposite? If so, can it be said that academic tenure has on the whole led to a decrease rather than to a genuine increase in academic freedom? This question is worth asking even though I have no good answer to it. In my opinion, it deserves further thought and serious investigation.

7/ The differences in *forgiving* between academia and non-academia parallel the differences in *salvation:* college professors rank both of these values as being far less important than do adult Americans. It can thus be said that college professors, at least in secular state universities, are less devout than the average American, at least in the way that organized Christian religions normally define devoutness.

8/ Finally, of special importance, college professors and adult Americans feel very differently about the importance of being *logical.* It is ranked seventeenth by the average adult American but fifth to eighth by the average college professor. The reason I think these findings deserve special notice is because contemporary social psychologists postulate a need for logical consistency and balance among cognitions to be a major motivating factor in human beings. The findings suggest, instead, that contemporary consistency and balance theories may be nothing more than projections of the college professor's values onto the man in the street. Logic and consistency seem to be distinctively academic values rather than universally held values.

Thus far, I have been discussing the value patterns characteristic of the Gowns and Towns of America, and, as I have already suggested, there is little reason to think that the value differences between the Gowns and Towns of Canada would be any different. Consider now the value patterns found for professors having different kinds of academic interests. I have arranged the five kinds of academic interests in Tables 1 and 2 in the order of their overall similarity to the national sample. Professors specializing in business have a value pattern that is the most similar to that of the national sample of adult Americans, followed by professors in the biological sciences, then the physical sciences, then the social sciences, followed, finally, by professors in the arts.

Notwithstanding these differences among academicians in different fields, it can nonetheless be observed that they are on the whole rather similar to one another, each of them being far more different from the national sample's value patterns than from one another's. There are, however, a few significant differences among the five academic areas which should be noted. Social scientists care more than do professors in the remaining disciplines for *equality, mature love*, and being *broadminded*, and they care less for *national security*. Professors in business rank *equality, a world of beauty*, and *wisdom* lower than do the others. Professors in the arts care more than do the others for *a world of beauty, wisdom*, and being *self-controlled*. Professors in the biological sciences seem to be more preoccupied with *national security* than the others and less preoccupied with *mature love* or with being *broadminded*. Finally, the only value that can be said to be peculiarly distinctive of professors in the physical sciences is that they place less importance than all the others on being *self-controlled*.

Our findings, then, reveal that professors in the different academic areas are distinguishable from one another in certain respects. This conclusion is consistent with findings of Nevitt Sanford's study in which lengthy interview rather than more terse psychometric procedures were employed as the main research tool. 'There is nothing to indicate,' Sanford writes (1970, p.18), 'that professors in psychology or other social science departments are different, on the significant dimensions, from professors in other departments. They are first of all academic men – participants in academic culture.' As already shown, the five academic groups are on the whole rather homogeneous in their value patterns, differing markedly from the national sample of adult Americans. Yet there are small differences, as I have already noted, social science professors on the whole having a greater disposition than their colleagues in other areas towards a liberal, tolerant and also a romantic personal outlook, and being somewhat less inclined towards a nationalistic outlook. On the basis of the latter finding, I would hazard the guess that the social-science departments of Canadian universities have recruited more foreign professors to their faculties than have non-social-science departments. A second prediction that would seem to flow from these data is that there should be more resistance to nationalistic hiring policies from Canadian social scientists than from other types of academicians.

A question may be raised as to whether the values of younger professors differ in any significant respects from those of older professors. It is reasonable to expect that a major determinant of academic values is socialization within the academic subculture, and that with increasing socialization academic values will become increasingly evident. But an analysis of the value rankings obtained for assistant, associate, and full professors shows remarkably similar value patterns. The differences are small in magnitude and there are only a very few statistically significant ones, few enough to suggest that they could easily have arisen by chance. It can thus be said that academic values are determined by selective factors that predispose certain people to enter an academic career, or by socialization to academic values in graduate school rather than after recruitment to faculty positions. These conjectures seem to be supported by data available for graduate students in psychology. I now turn to consider these data.

VALUES OF GRADUATE STUDENTS IN PSYCHOLOGY

Tables 3 and 4 display the comparable data available for a national sample of 937 graduate students in psychology whose average age was twenty-six. They were obtained from ninety-eight psychology departments across the United States, and they represent every field of interest in academic psychology. About two-thirds of them were men. Also shown, for comparative purposes, are the values obtained from a representative national sample of American adults between twenty-one and thirty years of age. It is reasonable to assume that the values exhibited by this sample of graduate students in psychology are at least roughly representative of graduate students in psychology everywhere, and perhaps to a somewhat lesser extent, of graduate students in other social-science disciplines. The data are taken from a recent paper by Silverman, Jaffe and Bishop (1972) and are reproduced here with their kind permission.

Compared with a national sample of Americans of the same age, graduate students in psychology seem to be less concerned with security – material security (*a comfortable life*), *family security*, *national security*, international security (*a world at peace*), and eternal security (*salvation*). They are, moreover, less concerned with the conventional values of *happiness*, being *ambitious, clean, obedient, polite, honest, forgiving, responsible, self-controlled.*

Instead, they seemed to care more about self-realization in their personal and work life. Compared with a national sample of their own age, they placed greater importance on a sense of *accomplishment, wisdom, inner harmony, self-respect, true friendship, mature love,* and on being *loving.* They care considerably more about being open to aesthetic, sensual, and intellectual experience (*a world of beauty, an exciting life, pleasure,* and being *broadminded*), intellectual competence (*capable, independent, intellectual,* and *logical*), and creativity (*imaginative*). And they are more concerned than the national group they are being compared with about being of service to their fellow man (being *helpful*).

Taking into account the age differences between graduate students and the college professors, it can be said that the overall pattern of values for this national sample of graduate students in psychology is basically similar to the value pattern found for college professors, except for the fact that the graduate students do not yet rank certain competence and self-realization values (for example, *a sense of accomplishment, being intellectual,* and *logical*) quite as high as professors do. But they care about as much as professors do about being *capable* and they care less than professors do about being *ambitious.* These differences notwithstanding, it is still apparent that the graduate students in psychology exhibit a value pattern that is far more similar to that exhibited by academicians than by the average American.

Now what about the values of undergraduate students?

UNDERGRADUATE VALUES

Tables 5 and 6 show the comparable value data that are presently available for undergraduate students in four countries – Canada, the United States, Australia and Israel. All four sets of data were obtained from undergraduate students enrolled in beginning (rather than advanced) psychology courses. I obtained the Canadian data at the University of Western Ontario, and the American data at Michigan State University. The Australian data were obtained by Feather (1970) at Flinders University in South Australia, and the Israeli data were obtained by Rim (1970) at the Israel Institute of Technology at Haifa. Only male undergraduates were tested in Israel, but both sexes are represented in the remaining three samples. Since the data shown in Tables 5 and 6 for the four national groups were collected by independent investigators having different purposes, direct statistical tests of significance of differences are not available. But a visual inspection of the value rankings obtained for the several samples is nonetheless informative, revealing many meaningful and often sizable differences among the undergraduates of the four countries. Of interest in the present context are not only the value differences found among the undergraduates in the four different countries but also the differences between undergraduate values and those of graduate students and professors.

The materialism-, competition-, and achievement-orientation which is so often attributed to Americans is manifested in the findings that male undergraduate Americans place relatively more importance than their counterparts in other countries on *a comfortable life, social recognition*, and being *ambitious*, and less importance on *equality* and on being *helpful*. Israelis rank *a world at peace* and *national security* first and second respectively in their value hierarchy — for geopolitical reasons which are perhaps self-evident, Israelis care more about being *capable* than about being *ambitious*, and they care considerably more than do undergraduates in Canada, the United States, and Australia about being *intellectual* and *logical*. And not surprisingly, Israeli undergraduates place least importance on the the two values — *salvation* and *forgiving* — that previous research has identified as being the most distinctively Christian values (Rokeach 1969).

Australian undergraduates seem to be most notably different from undergraduates in the other countries in their higher rankings of *true friendship*, which is consistent with what several observers of Australia have reported about 'mateship' being a distinctively Australian value (Lipset 1963). Australian undergraduates also differ from undergraduates in the other three countries in placing more importance on *equality, a sense of accomplishment, wisdom*, and on being *broadminded*.

Perhaps most interesting in the present context, and perhaps most disturbing too, are the findings about the values of Canadian undergraduates tested at the University of Western Ontario. The most striking finding is that these undergraduate men and women seem to place less importance than do undergraduates in the United States, Australia, and Israel on *a sense of accomplishment*, on being *ambitious* and *capable*, and on being *logical* and *self-controlled. A sense of accomplishment* is ranked ninth by Canadian men and women, *ambitious* and *capable* are ranked eleventh or twelfth, and *self-controlled* and *logical* are ranked thirteenth and fourteenth respectively. In contrast, undergraduates in the other three countries, especially male undergraduates, typically assign higher rankings to these values.

If these Canadian undergraduates do not seem to be overly preoccupied with self-realization through achievement and intellectual competence, what are they preoccupied with? The data suggests that they are concerned with more personal kinds of self-realization – love, peace of mind, personal happiness, and in the case of Canadian men, with being free and independent.

Seymour Lipset writes that 'Canada is lower than the United States on ... egalitarianism [and] achievement ... Geography, too, inhibited the spread of egalitarianism and individualism on the Canadian Frontier ... add to this a self-serving elite – that gain by keeping close ties to the Mother Country – deliberately playing down egalitarianism and individualism ... ' (1963, pp.521-2). And Lipset quotes Kaspar Naegele: 'There seems to be less optimism, less faith in the future, less willingness to risk capital or reputation. In contrast to America, Canada is a country of greater caution, reserve, and restraint' (p.522).

Tables 5 and 6 show that undergraduate Canadian men care somewhat more for *equality, freedom,* and *independence* than their American counterparts, while undergraduate Canadian women care somewhat less for these three values. There is thus no support here for Lipset's hypothesis that Canadians are less egalitarian or individualistic than Americans. There is support, however, for his hypothesis that Canadians are less achievement- and competence-oriented, although it is by no means clear that these arise, as Lipset intimates, from a lack of optimism or faith in the future, or from a greater 'caution, reserve, or restraint'. It is entirely possible that the particular value patterns obtained for the Canadian undergraduates reflect instead a deliberate rejection of achievement and competence values in favour of a greater preference for other personal values. Further research is needed, however, to determine which of these alternative interpretations is the more plausible.

SOME REFLECTIONS ABOUT IMPROVING
UNDERGRADUATE AND GRADUATE TRAINING

It is reasonable to conclude from the data I have reported that the values of the academic community are distinctively different from the values of the society at large. It is also reasonably clear that the values of undergraduates in the several countries studied, particularly the values of Canadian undergraduates, deviate in certain important respects from those obtained for graduate students, particularly with respect to competence values, and deviate even more markedly from the value patterns obtained for faculty. Put somewhat differently, the findings suggest a smaller value gap between faculty members and graduate students, and a larger one between faculty and undergraduate students, the size of this gap varying with the nationality of the undergraduate students under consideration. Assuming for the moment that all these data, notwithstanding the fact that they have been brought together here from such widely divergent sources, are nonetheless at least roughly representative of the values of the three main academic groupings in any major university (an assumption which will surely require additional empirical investigation), they suggest at the least that a major part of the problem we face in attempting to improve the quality of undergraduate education may stem from the relatively large value gap existing between faculty and undergraduate students.

In contrast, the data do not suggest cause for a similar concern with regard to improving graduate education. Here, our main concern seems to be a somewhat different one: to what extent is our graduate education organized and designed to facilitate the further development and realization of already existing academic values? This question touches not only upon the organization and quality of graduate education but also upon the organization and quality of faculty life, the organization and quality of our respective disciplines, and of intradisciplinary and interdisciplinary associations as well.

It is not possible on an occasion such as this to address oneself systematically to the many complex issues which I have touched upon concerning the quality of life as it exists in an academic environment. All I can hope to do in the present context is to offer a few selected 'pet' reflections about improving the quality of undergraduate and graduate training in the social sciences.

Selection of undergraduate students

The data suggest that perhaps too many undergraduates are being recruited to the University, whose values are incompatible with academic values, and that more stringent selection procedures may be required to weed out those with value patterns grossly incompatible with academic values. To one extent or another, and by one means or another, probably most academic institutions already employ such selection procedures, either in advance or within a short time after recruitment to the University. But the more we move away from an elitist philosophy of higher education to embrace a more democratic philosophy of equal opportunity, a limit is necessarily placed on the extent to which rigorous selection procedures can become the main method for improving the quality of life within the academic environment. We must face the fact, increasingly, that undergraduates attend university because of many motivations rather than just a single motivation: not only to study and to learn and to develop new intellectual skills, but also to prepare for some vocation, to meet new friends, to make lasting and useful social contacts, to find a mate, to enjoy all the conveniences of freedom and independence in being away from home but none of the inconveniences; and, I suppose too, to engage in all the joyful and sorrowful youthful activities that undergraduates have traditionally engaged in. All such diverse motivations are organized in different students into a priority system, and they are cognitively manifested and justified, to oneself and to others, in terms of one or another hierarchical value pattern.

Given the fact that higher education in democratic countries is becoming increasingly a higher education for the masses, perhaps we had best take undergraduate students as they come to us, with all their multi-faceted motivations, and do the best we can to educate them. In other words, we must at the least, find better methods for teaching course content and, perhaps equally important, we must find ways of *changing* their value priorities – by raising their values for self-actualization, competence, and excellence (or whatever names one might choose), on the assumption that such changes in value priorities will predispose them to become more receptive to whatever the university might have to offer them.

Value change as an educational objective

Not all educators would necessarily agree that academic institutions are or should be in the business of promoting or changing certain values. Some would argue that the halls and classrooms of academia must remain value-free, that the University should transmit its knowledge and impart its skills to those who already have the right kind of values, to those who already have a strong enough motivation to learn. I would argue, instead, that every society 'assigns' a dual mission to its educational institutions: on the one hand, to produce and transmit the knowledge acquired by one generation to succeeding generations, and on the other, to transmit and inculcate succeeding generations of students with certain values that are its specialized concern. These two kinds of functions are of course highly interrelated: the inculcation of certain kinds of values are seen as facilitating the student's acquisition of substantive knowledge and skills.

As previously suggested, the educational institution is not the only institution of society in the business of shaping and changing values. The family, the church, and the military, for instance, all see themselves as being legitimately concerned with the promotion of certain subsets of values, in directions that are congruent with their respective 'institutional values'. Parents, clergymen, and military men alike would all like to think that their role performances do indeed significantly affect the values of those in their charge, and consider themselves competent to the extent they see themselves as succeeding in doing so. In the same way, teachers, who are the agents of the educational institution, take professional pride in their teaching to the extent that they see it as affecting in some significant way not only the knowledge and skills but also the values of their students.

Relevance of social science courses

The values that undergraduate students possess are, of course, major determinants of their perceptions of what is relevant and irrelevant, significant and trivial in course content. The word 'relevance' has been used in at least four different ways in educational circles: personal relevance, social relevance, technological relevance, and theoretical relevance. The knowledge of social science may be perceived to be relevant by a student as far as it helps him understand himself, or as far as it helps him to understand better the society he lives in, or as far as he sees it having some useful application to the solution of some social problem, or as far as he preceives it to be relevant for advancing his theoretical understanding and knowledge. Given the differences in values between undergraduate and graduate students, it seems unlikely that they will appreciate in the same way the relevance or significance of the social science courses they take. An appreciation of theory-oriented courses presupposes one kind of value system, and an appreciation of problem-oriented courses presupposes some other kind of value system.

Increasingly, we hear undergraduate students complain that they do not perceive the university and the courses they take as relevant. The more militant the student the more likely that he will be impatient with theoretical relevance and the more likely that he will articulate relevance to mean the application of knowledge to the solution of the ills of society — war, poverty, racism, sexism, unemployment, drug abuse, the increasing crime rate, and the like. This type of demand for relevance, which I have called technological relevance, has in recent years become increasingly reinforced by professional and scientific societies, university administrations, faculty members themselves, and most recently, by fund-granting agencies. In practice, however, those who clamour for such relevance are often content to settle for the somewhat less stringent kinds of relevance that I have mentioned — the extent to which the knowledge produced by the social sciences helps us at least to *understand* what is going on in ourselves and in society, even if practical solutions to our own and society's ills are not immediately forthcoming.

But I suspect that the most important kinds of relevance for the average undergraduate, who is neither especially militant nor articulate, are *personal* and *social* relevance. To him relevance means that what he learns from his social-science courses increases self-awareness and an awareness of others, a broader and deeper understanding of his own and others' motivations, and how his personality and character might have become shaped by society, family, genetic endowment and personal experience.

Increasing numbers of students in recent years have enrolled in social science courses, especially in psychology courses, because they are motivated by the desire to understand themselves and others better, in order to resolve personal conflicts, reduce anxiety, increase their ability to relate harmoniously with others, and hopefully, also to apply (or, as many undergraduates would say, *use*) such knowledge afterwards in their daily work and family life. The textbooks they are assigned and the lectures they are asked to attend contain what must appear to the undergraduate student to be countless bewildering reports about causal and correlational relationships among cultural, sociological, demo-graphic, situational, personological, cognitive, behavioural, and genetic variables, as these have been demonstrated in empirical research with *others*. Undergraduate students are expected to learn about such relationships and are tested for their knowledge about them on the assumption, no doubt, that such knowledge will increase their under-standing not only of others but also themselves. But, paradoxically, great pains are usually taken to prevent students from finding out about their own position on the social and personal variables they learn about in their textbooks and lectures. Keeping students in the dark about their own position on such variables may be tantamount to throwing away our best teaching tool – the motivation that comes from social and especially personal relevance – a teaching advantage that the natural sciences do not possess. The way psychology and the other social sciences are typically taught discourages students from making personal applications of empirical knowledge. Thus they stand little chance of discovering whether they are, for instance, high, middle, or low on prejudice as compared with others, or, that they are authoritarian, dogmatic, rigid, Machievellian, aggressive, achievement- or affiliation-oriented, externally or internally controlled, intolerant of ambiguity, repressed, impulsive, extraverted, neurotic or psychopathic. Few students ever get to find out about their own IQ scores, or their own scores on tests of interests, abilities, attitudes, values, or on pro-jective tests or other personality tests. Whatever they might learn about such things they learn about others and it is all far removed from themselves.

There is an almost complete consensus among psychologists that students in general and 'clients' in particular should not be informed about their performance on such psychological tests as intelligence, personality, and projective tests, on the grounds that such results would be 'subject to misuse in the hands of non-professionals' (*APA Monitor*, 1972, p.17). An alternative view that I wish to propose is that the main danger comes not so much from non-professionals who might 'misuse' such information, but from professionals who are not inclined to go to the bother of explaining to non-professionals, in non-technical language, what their test scores really mean. No wonder students taking social science courses often complain that their courses are not relevant.

Beyond the question of self-knowledge about single variables there is the further question of self-knowledge about relationships that are found to exist between two or more variables. Relationships between psychological variables are *always* far from perfect, which means that there must necessarily always be some individuals who will fall into the 'wrong' cells. Because we do not give students in psychology courses (and also in other social-science courses) the opportunity of finding out about such empirical relationships, as *such relationships might exist within thier own psychological makeups*, we pass up many precious teaching and change-inducing opportunities. Examples of such opportunities would be, confronting a student with the fact that he scores high in need achievement yet is doing poorly in school; or that he scores average in intelligence yet is striving for a PhD; or that he scores high in anti-Semitism yet scores low in authoritarianism (or vice versa); or that he scores high in aesthetic interest yet had not attended an art exhibition or concert all year; or that he scores high in need for independence yet had succumbed to the social pressures of a Sherif-, or Asch-, or Milgram-type experiment that he had participated in; or that he is a frequent church-goer yet compassionate only to the poor and the sick of his own community who are white. All such personal kinds of knowledge are typically ruled out as not being relevant to the theoretical understanding of relationships, perhaps on the assumption that social-science principles must be learned and understood in the same detached way we learn and understand the principle of gravity, the laws of logic, and the periodic tables.

What evidence is there to suggest that making the content of social-science courses personally relevant is a more effective way of teaching than the more conventional methods? Research findings to date (Rokeach 1968, 1971, 1973) indicate that undergraduate students undergo long-term changes in their values, attitudes, and behaviour as a result of feedback of social-science information that is made personally relevant by allowing them to compare their own positions on measured variables with those of others. By long-term changes I mean changes that are observed as long as twenty-one months after a single feedback. Thus, students who discover that they are pro-civil-rights in their social attitude (when compared to others) yet anti-*equality* in their value (when compared to others) will increase their regard for *equality* and will, moreover, be significantly more likely to engage in egalitarian behaviour, such as responding positively to a solicitation for membership in a civil-rights organization. Undergraduate students who discover that their regard for *a world of beauty* is lower than that accorded this value by other college students will increase their regard for *a world of beauty* and will furthermore undergo change in other ecology-related attitudes (Hollen 1972). Undergraduate students who discover that certain of their own values are more similar to the values of the uneducated than to those of the educated will undergo long-term changes in these values in order to bring them into closer alignment with those of the educated. Undergraduate students who discover that certain of their values are more characteristic of the elderly than of the young will undergo change in these values in order to bring them into closer alignment with the values that are characteristic of the young. All such findings suggest that personally relevant information can and does affect the student, not because the average undergraduate is necessarily motivated to conform slavishly to the values and attitudes of his peers, but because the information is seen to violate self-conceptions about competence or morality. Other findings (Lundy 1972) suggest that social-science data which are made personally relevant are better recalled on final examinations than are identical data presented in a manner which is not personally relevant.

From relevance to excellence
Beyond the challenges we face of making our social science courses more personally, socially, and technologically relevant lies a deeper challenge: to train our students, graduate and undergraduate, to appreciate social-science knowledge for its theoretical relevance. This seems to me to be the essence of university training for excellence. At the

graduate level in psychology, and I suspect also in other social-science disciplines, we seem to be more successful in training research technicians than analytic thinkers who can appreciate the theoretically significant from the theoretically trivial (Proshansky 1972). Even at graduate levels we seem to be more successful in training students to become question answerers than question askers (Rokeach 1965).

Einstein once said that to ask a question is to answer it. In a *Life* magazine article Szilard noted: 'The most important step in getting a job done is the recognition of a problem. Once I recognize a problem I usually can think of someone who can work it out better than I could' (1961, p.75). Similarly, Hadamard has said: 'Before trying to discover anything ... there arises the question: What shall we try to discover? What problems shall we try to solve?' (1945, p.124).

But a peculiar division of labour has long existed between teachers and students. On examinations and in the lecture hall it is the professor who traditionally plays the role of asking the questions, and the student the role of answering them, as if to suggest that the quality of education is to be sought in the answers rather than the questions. Thus, we will often hear professors complaining about the quality of the answers they receive to their examination questions, but rarely will we hear complaints or doubts raised about the quality of the questions that professors ask. My point is that students are not being trained and are rarely examined for their ability to ask questions, in contrast to our relentless examinations of their ability to answer questions.

Learning how to formulate significant questions is again a question of values, and it is also a skill that most of us probably are unable to teach. Hadamard has suggested that the sense of beauty can inform us. Others speak of scientific taste, or literary taste, or artistic taste. Taste and beauty, as well as elegance, parsimony, and comprehensiveness are values that are recognized and appreciated by men of culture, education, and science. Thus, to train students to ask significant questions will require more than merely making our courses personally relevant, or even socially and technologically relevant. For beyond all these kinds of relevance lies theoretical relevance. All these kinds of relevance are ultimately related, and one can even suspect that they are hierarchically arranged. Kurt Lewin has said this much better: 'There is nothing more practical than a good theory.'

I hope that the new Social Science Centre will be able to play a significant role in sensitizing graduate students and also undergraduate students to appreciate the intimate connections that must surely exist among the four kinds of relevance that I have discussed here.

SOME REFLECTIONS ABOUT INTRADISCIPLINARY AND INTERDISCIPLINARY ASSOCIATIONS

In this section I would like to offer a few highly selected and general observations about the present state of psychology and, also, about its relation to other disciplines. The total field of psychology can no longer be easily characterized or grasped in its entirety since it includes too many specialties and subspecialties, too many 'middle range' theories which are in quite rapid states of flux. The good old days of a few grand theories – psychoanalysis, Gestalt psychology, field theory and learning theory – seem long gone, having given way to many different varieties and subvarieties of personality, cognitive, and behaviour theories. One thing that these theories seem to have in common is that they all share a common concern with one or another set of conditions leading to change. But the kinds of change that the various psychological theories are focused upon are highly diversified – for instance, personality change, cognitive change, motivational change, attitude change, value change, developmental change, structural change, and behavioural change. And beyond all these different kinds of change that psychologists talk about, there are the theories of change that the other social science disciplines are concerned with – for instance, social and political change, economic and ecological change, institutional and cultural change.

The various theories in contemporary psychology differ not only in the kinds of change they are most concerned with but also in the methods advocated to bring about change, in the specificity or generality of change, and in the ease or difficulty of assessing change. They are not so much *competing* theories, offering alternative interpretations of the same phenomena, as theories that supplement or complement one another, that is, theories that address themselves to, attempt to understand and explain different psychological phenomena.

None of the theories of personality, social psychology, and behaviourism can be regarded as comprehensive theories of change. A comprehensive theory should ideally be able to specify the conditions that will lead to behavioural change as well as to cognitive and personality change, to cognitive change as well as to personality change, to long-term change as well as to short-term change, to a raising or lowering of self-conceptions as well as to their mere maintenance. A more integrated theory of psychology requires a theoretical framework that at least attempts to bridge the gaps that presently exist among the various theories which, for the most part, are not on speaking terms with one another, more or less going their separate ways and ignoring one another. Moreover, we are now witnessing a proliferation of highly specialized, compartmentalized theories and models that are invented *ad hoc* to deal with highly circumscribed sets of empirical findings. One may note more reluctance nowadays to deal with broad theoretical issues, and a greater reluctance to tackle the always difficult task of theoretical integration or synthesis of psychological knowledge. And all this seems somehow to be manifested in our graduate teaching, at the least, in our overemphasis on methodological sophistication at the expense of theoretical sophistication. As Jacob Viner is reported to have put it in a recent issue of *Contemporary Psychology* (January 1973): 'Men are not narrow in their intellectual interests by nature; it takes special and vigorous training to accomplish that end' (p.27).

Actually, I would suggest that many theories of personality and therapy and behaviour are *balance* theories of change, in the same sense that social psychologists speak of cognitive theories as consistency or balance theories. Therefore, instead of ignoring one another as they now do they can be compared and integrated with one another, to ascertain, at least, in what sense they are balance theories, and to what extent they might overlap with one another. Psychoanalysis, which in my opinion is the earliest of the balance theories, seeks to bring about personality change by exposing *contradictions* between id, ego, and superego to conscious awareness. Rational (Ellis 1962) and reality (Glasser 1965) therapy and emotional role-playing (Janis and Mann 1965; Mann and Janis 1968) attempt to bring about changes in personality by confronting a person with *contradictions* between self-conceptions and behaviour. Non-directive therapy (Rogers 1959) attempts to bring about personality change by confronting the client with *contradictions* between self-conceptions and the unqualified positive regard for the client by the therapist. Encounter groups (Burton 1969), sensitivity groups (Campbell and Dunnette 1968), and psychodrama (Moreno 1946) all attempt to bring about personality change by making a person aware of contradictions between self-conceptions and conceptions about the needs and values of other people.

In contrast to such theories of personality and therapy, cognitive theories in social psychology and behavioural-modification theories are more modest in aim, seeking to change specific behaviours, attitudes, or values. Bandura's theory of modelling and observational learning (1969) seeks to bring about a specified behavioural change by confronting a person with the *contradiction* between the rewards he perceives himself obtaining and his image of those gained by a successful model. Most cognitive theories of change in social psychology are primarily balance theories concerning attitude change; they are not especially concerned with personality change or even with behavioural change. They seek to bring about attitude change by confronting the person with a *contradiction* between an attitude and behaviour, or between two attitudes, or between a person's own attitudes and those held by a 'significant other'. For a more detailed discussion of the similarities and differences among these cognitive theories of change, as well as their similarities and differences to personality and behavioural theories of change, see Rokeach (1973).

It will perhaps be enough to note here that virtually all theories of personality and therapy attempt to induce enduring change by making a person aware of one or another type of contradiction that chronically exists within the person below his level of awareness. These contradictions always implicate self-conceptions about one's competence or morality, and insight into such contradictions is believed to lead to personality change. The aim of the theories is education and re-education (Lewin and Grabbe 1945) rather than merely persuasion; enhancement of the self-concept rather than merely its maintenance; growth and self-actualization rather than a mere removal of imbalanced states or a mere return to previous states of balance.

In contrast, cognitively oriented theories in social psychology have typically remained unconcerned about changes in personality or self-conceptions because these variables are considered to be too complex, too central, or too ill-defined to be amenable to demonstrate change as a result of situational and experimental variation. Instead they have concentrated on short-lived cognitive changes rather than on enduring personality changes. And in contrast to theories of personality and therapy, cognitive theories in social psychology have not concerned themselves with whether an attitude change merely restores an earlier state of consistency or represents a higher or lower, more or less integrated, mature, or self-actualized level of consistency. And because these theories in social psychology have been indifferent to such issues, they have for the most part been ignored as irrelevant by personality psychologists, humanistic psychologists and psychologists who practise therapy.

The kind of change that behavioural theories are mostly concerned with is, of course, behavioural change. Traditionally, behaviour theorists have rejected cognitive and personality approaches to change as too mentalistic and therefore unscientific or nonexistent (an exception might perhaps be made of Bandura's theory of observational learning). The kind of change they normally deal with is necessarily limited to behaviour and such theories are not claimed to lead to changes in attitudes, or values, or self-conceptions, or personality (Skinner 1971).

All the preceding remarks are intended to break down at least a few of the barriers to theoretical integration which can presently be discerned within the discipline of psychology. It would be surprising, in view of this intradisciplinary fragmentation and compartmentalization, if there were not also some glaring communication gaps across disciplines. This lack of communication is most evident, to me at least, in the typical relation between faculty and graduate students who have received their social-psychological training within psychology departments on the one hand and within sociology departments on the other. In both of these disciplines, social psychology has long been a field of specialization — for well over half a century. The Division of Personality and Social Psychology (Division 8) is the largest single division within the American Psychological Association. Stehr and Larson inform us that for sociologists: 'The most frequently listed area of specialization in 1970 was social psychology. It was listed by almost every fifth member of the American Sociological Association and was listed almost twice as often as the second area of specialization, methodology and statistics' (1972, p.5). These figures notwithstanding we will rarely find social psychologists trained in psychology who know what their colleagues in sociology are doing, and vice versa. Graduate students in sociology specializing in social psychology rarely register for the social-psychology courses offered by the psychology department of their university, and vice versa. A major reason for all this isolation, I suppose, is that the two social psychologies favour somewhat different theories (for example, symbolic interaction vs cognitive interaction) and different methods (for example, experimental methods vs survey and field research). Typically, neither kind of social psychologist finds that what the other has to offer is directly relevant to his own interests, except in some highly peripheral or tangential way. This state of intellectual isolation is, in my experience, typical in Canadian as well as in American universities. On the occasion of the official opening of this Social Science Centre which is intended to provide a common home for all the social sciences, it is perhaps not inappropriate to suggest a closer examination of the historical and contemporary reasons for this isolation between two social science subdisciplines which share so common a substantive interest, and a closer examination of whether this isolation facilitates or hinders the realization of the values distinctive of academia in general and the social sciences in particular.

I will conclude this section with the reflection – rather, the suspicion – that psychologists in other areas of specialization will probably be able to point to similar instances of compartmentalization among various subdisciplines within psychology, and between psychology and other fields sharing common interests in the natural and social sciences. In my own view, the unity of all the social sciences can perhaps best be advanced by focusing on two main theoretical issues – the common interest that they all share in the issue of change, as has been noted, and the common interest that they all have in the antecedents of consequences of human values. A focus on these two issues leads one to ask additional questions that might serve the cause of intradisciplinary and interdisciplinary collaboration. What kinds of change are the main concerns within and between the social science disciplines? How are these various and diverse kinds of change brought about? Can they be systematically related to one another? Exactly what interest does a particular social science discipline have in human values? Are values conceived as the independent or dependent variables in the various social science disciplines? And exactly which values are of main concern to the various social sciences?

SOME NEGLECTED AREAS OF RESEARCH WITHIN A CANADIAN CONTEXT

Finally, a few brief comments are in order about some areas of research in psychology that might be especially appropriate within the Canadian cultural context. While there can be no distinctively Canadian psychology for the same reason that there can be no distinctively black or Jewish or Soviet psychology (or sociology, or economics, etc.), it is likely that certain problems can more readily be investigated within a particular cultural or social context, and it would be useful to try to identify at least a few problems that can be more easily studied in one particular country rather than another. One example that comes to mind is the Canadian research on second-language acquisition (Gardner and Lambert 1972). In the same vein, it is likely that there are several other problem areas that might be more readily pursued within a Canadian context.

Gordon (1964) has identified seven stages of migrant assimilation, and drawing on this work, Feather and Wasyluk, in South Australia (1973, in press), have investigated 'the internal or subjective changes that can be assumed to go on in the cognitive sphere as the migrant's (Ukrainian's) values, attitudes, and ways of thinking come to resemble those of his host culture' (p.3). It seems to me that the contemporary Canadian cultural context provides the social scientist with an even more suitable natural laboratory for the systematic study of processes of cultural assimilation and related processes of socialization.

We have heard a good deal recently, within the Canadian context, about the issues of separatism and *deux nations*. In exactly what sense can it be said that Canada consists of two nations or cultures? Is it possible to identify the specific values that English and French Canadians hold in common and the specific values that differentiate them from one another? *Which* value differences would the English and French Canadians care most about and thus most wish to preserve and which ones would they care less about? How would one go about perpetuating or eliminating whatever value differences there may turn out to be between English and French Canadians? I believe that research dealing with such problems would be highly timely and might lead not only to advances in theoretical knowledge but also to the alleviation of this thorny sociopolitical problem.

More generally, perhaps, Canada provides a natural laboratory for the cross-validation of various theories concerning intergroup relations, prejudice, and discrimination. Anderson and Côté (1966), and Martin (1964) have shown that the principle of belief congruence as a determinant of discrimination (a principle which states that differences in beliefs and values are more important determinants of discrimination than differences in race or ethnic membership) is just as valid in the Canadian context as in the American context. Parallel perhaps to the problems of institutional racism and sexism in the United States, Canada probably has many of the same problems except that the particular ethnic and racial groups are differet. To what extent, we may ask, are the forces for segregation and desegregation of white and black Americans in the United States similar to and different from the forces for separatism and integration among the French, Indian, and English Canadians? To what extent can prejudice against certain racial and ethnic groups be learned or socially legitimated in the absence of direct intergroup contact, via invasions of such mass-media programs as *All in the Family* (Vidmar and Rokeach 1973)? To what extent can it be said that the social forces leading to genocide among the Ihalmiut – the inland Eskimos of Canada's Barrens (Mowat 1968) – are similar to and different from the social forces leading to genocide and other socially legitimated evils (Sanford 1972) in South Africa and Rhodesia, in Hitler's Germany, Stalin's Russia, and America's Vietnam?

I hope that the Social Science Centre at the University of Western Ontario will soon come to symbolize not only a house but also a home for all the social scientists who are occupying it. But as everyone knows, if this or any other domicile is to be converted from a house to a home special added effort is usually required.

TABLE 1

Terminal value medians and composite rank orders for five academic fields and for adult Americans

	Adult Americans N = 1409	Business 38	Biological science 51
A comfortable life (a prosperous life)	9.0(9)	11.8(13)	14.8(16)
An exciting life (a stimulating, active life)	15.3(18)	9.8(9)	9.2(8)
A sense of accomplishment (lasting contribution)	9.0(10)	5.0(3)	2.8(1)
A world at peace (free of war and conflict)	3.3(1)	8.3(6)	7.1(6)
A world of beauty (beauty of nature and the arts)	13.6(15)	13.5(14)	11.3(12)
Equality (brotherhood, equal opportunity for all)	8.5(7)	8.9(7)	7.2(7)
Family security (taking care of loved ones)	3.8(2)	4.2(1)	5.1(4)
Freedom (independence, free choice)	5.5(3)	4.8(2)	6.4(5)
Happiness (contentedness)	7.6(4)	9.8(10)	10.6(11)
Inner harmony (freedom from inner conflict)	10.5(13)	9.3(8)	9.4(9)
Mature love (sexual and spiritual intimacy)	12.5(14)	10.5(11)	11.6(13)
National security (protection from attack)	9.5(12)	14.5(17)	13.7(15)
Pleasure (an enjoyable, leisurely life)	14.6(17)	14.3(15)	16.1(17)
Salvation (saved, eternal life)	8.8(8)	15.5(18)	17.3(18)
Self-respect (self-esteem)	7.7(5)	5.5(4)	4.3(2)
Social recognition (respect, admiration)	14.4(16)	14.5(16)	12.9(14)
True friendship (close companionship)	9.3(11)	11.5(12)	9.8(10)
Wisdom (a mature understanding of life)	8.0(6)	5.8(5)	5.0(3)

Figures shown are median rankings and, in parentheses, composite rank orders.

TABLE I

Physical science 51	Social science 50	Arts 22	p*	p**
14.7(15)	14.9(15)	14.1(15)	.001	–
8.0(7)	8.5(8)	12.5(14)	.001	–
4.0(1)	3.3(1)	3.2(2)	.001	–
9.0(9)	7.3(7)	8.0(6)	.001	–
10.3(11)	11.3(12)	7.0(5)	.001	–
8.4(8)	5.0(3)	8.0(7)	.001	.001
5.3(4)	5.5(5)	8.5(8)	.001	–
4.3(2)	5.7(6)	8.5(9)	.–	.05
11.8(13)	12.3(13)	11.2(12)	.001	–
7.3(6)	9.0(9)	4.8(3)	.01	–
9.6(10)	9.3(10)	9.5(10)	.001	–
15.3(17)	16.5(17)	15.5(17)	.001	.05
14.9(16)	15.1(16)	14.8(16)	–	–
17.7(18)	17.6(18)	17.7(18)	.001	–
5.0(3)	4.3(2)	5.5(4)	.001	–
14.3(14)	12.3(14)	12.5(13)	.01	–
11.1(12)	11.1(11)	11.0(11)	.01	–
5.6(5)	5.3(4)	1.5(1)	.001	.01

* Comparing all six groups   ** Comparing five academic groups only

TABLE 2

Instrumental value medians and composite rank orders for five academic fields
and for adult Americans

	Adult Americans N = 1409	Business 38	Biological science 51
Ambitious (hard-working, aspiring)	6.5(2)	7.8(8)	7.1(6)
Broadminded (open-minded)	7.5(5)	7.5(6)	8.9(9)
Capable (competent, effective)	9.5(9)	6.5(3)	6.6(5)
Cheerful (lighthearted, joyful)	9.9(12)	13.1(15)	12.8(14)
Clean (neat, tidy)	8.7(8)	16.0(17)	15.7(17)
Courageous (standing up for your beliefs)	7.8(6)	7.8(7)	6.4(4)
Forgiving (willing to pardon others)	7.2(4)	11.5(14)	11.1(12)
Helpful (working for the welfare of others)	8.2(7)	9.5(11)	10.0(11)
Honest (sincere, truthful)	3.3(1)	3.8(1)	3.2(1)
Imaginative (daring, creative)	15.4(18)	9.0(10)	8.4(8)
Independent (self-reliant, self-sufficient)	10.5(13)	8.0(9)	9.0(10)
Intellectual (intelligent, reflective)	13.0(15)	6.5(4)	6.3(3)
Logical (consistent, rational)	14.2(17)	7.5(5)	7.6(7)
Loving (affectionate, tender)	9.7(11)	11.5(13)	13.3(15)
Obedient (dutiful, respectful)	13.3(16)	17.0(18)	16.7(18)
Polite (courteous, well-mannered)	10.8(14)	15.0(16)	14.0(16)
Responsible (dependable, reliable)	6.7(3)	6.2(2)	4.8(2)
Self-controlled (restrained, self-disciplined)	9.6(10)	10.5(12)	11.4(13)

Figures shown are median rankings and, in parentheses, composite rank orders.

TABLE 2

Physical science 51	Social science 50	Arts 22	p*	p**
9.6(11)	10.5(11)	11.5(12)	.001	–
6.1(2)	5.0(1)	6.2(5)	.05	.05
6.3(3)	5.4(3)	6.3(6)	.001	–
12.8(15)	13.9(15)	14.0(15)	.001	–
15.9(17)	16.5(17)	16.6(18)	.001	–
7.3(6)	8.0(9)	9.2(10)	–	–
10.7(12)	11.1(13)	11.5(13)	.001	–
9.6(10)	9.2(10)	10.9(11)	.01	–
3.3(1)	5.2(2)	4.5(2)	–	–
6.6(5)	7.0(5)	6.0(3)	.001	–
8.0(9)	7.5(7)	8.9(9)	.001	–
6.4(4)	5.7(4)	4.0(1)	.001	–
7.6(8)	7.8(8)	6.5(7)	.001	–
11.3(13)	11.0(12)	12.8(14)	–	–
17.6(18)	17.3(18)	15.5(17)	.001	–
15.5(16)	15.5(16)	14.9(16)	.001	–
7.3(7)	7.0(6)	6.0(4)	–	–
12.7(14)	11.5(14)	8.2(8)	.001	.05

* Comparing all six groups   ** Comparing five academic groups only

TABLE 3

Terminal value medians and composite rank orders for psychology graduate students and adult Americans 21 - 30 years old

	Psychology graduate students N = 937	Adults 21 - 30 N = 251	Significance
A comfortable life	13.9(16)	9.6(9)	.01
An exciting life	8.9(11)	15.2(18)	.01
A sense of accomplishment	7.4(8)	9.0(8)	.01
A world at peace	7.2(5)	3.9(2)	.01
A world of beauty	12.0(13)	14.0(15)	.01
Equality	8.1(9)	8.0(6)	–
Family security	9.8(12)	3.9(1)	.01
Freedom	5.4(2)	4.3(3)	.01
Happiness	8.3(10)	7.1(4)	.01
Inner harmony	7.3(7)	11.0(14)	.01
Mature love	5.4(1)	10.0(12)	.01
National security	16.5(17)	9.9(11)	.01
Pleasure	13.3(14)	14.6(17)	.01
Salvation	17.8(18)	9.6(10)	.01
Self-respect	5.5(3)	8.4(7)	.01
Social recognition	13.3(15)	14.4(16)	.01
True friendship	7.3(6)	10.0(13)	.01
Wisdom	6.7(4)	7.7(5)	.05

Figures shown are median rankings, and in parentheses, composite rank orders.

TABLE 4

Instrumental value medians and composite rank orders for psychology graduate
students and adult Americans 21 - 30 years old

	Psychology graduate students N = 937	Adults 21 - 30 N = 251	Significance
Ambitious	12.1(14)	7.8(4)	.01
Broadminded	5.6(3)	8.1(5)	.01
Capable	6.0(4)	10.5(13)	.01
Cheerful	11.5(13)	11.1(14)	–
Clean	16.9(17)	8.3(7)	.01
Courageous	8.6(10)	8.7(8)	–
Forgiving	10.3(12)	7.5(3)	.01
Helpful	8.0(9)	9.6(10)	.01
Honest	4.8(1)	3.3(1)	.01
Imaginative	7.1(7)	15.1(18)	.01
Independent	6.0(5)	10.4(12)	.01
Intellectual	7.0(6)	12.3(15)	.01
Logical	10.2(11)	13.8(17)	.01
Loving	4.9(2)	8.1(6)	.01
Obedient	17.6(18)	13.0(16)	.01
Polite	15.4(16)	10.2(11)	.01
Responsible	7.2(8)	5.5(2)	.01
Self-controlled	13.1(15)	9.5(9)	.01

Figures shown are median rankings, and in parentheses, composite rank orders.

TABLE 5

Terminal value medians and composite rank orders for Canadian, American, and Australian college men and women, and for Israeli college men

	Men				Women		
	Canadian N = 125	American N = 169	Australian N = 279	Israeli N = 71	Canadian N = 133	American N = 129	Australian N = 184
A comfortable life	11.6(13)	10.3(11)	12.6(13)	12.8(15)	12.5(14)	13.8(16)	13.9(16)
An exciting life	9.8(11)	10.8(12)	9.2(11)	8.7(9)	10.7(11)	13.3(14)	10.2(12)
A sense of accomplishment	9.2(9)	7.1(5)	6.3(4)	7.5(7)	10.5(9)	8.2(9)	6.8(7)
A world at peace	10.0(12)	9.3(10)	8.2(9)	4.7(1)	10.8(12)	7.5(8)	6.2(4)
A world of beauty	12.3(15)	14.4(18)	13.0(15)	14.5(17)	12.3(13)	12.8(13)	11.9(13)
Equality	9.7(10)	12.3(13)	9.0(10)	9.3(10)	10.6(10)	8.4(10)	7.9(10)
Family security	7.5(7)	8.1(7)	9.5(12)	7.9(8)	8.8(8)	8.8(11)	8.3(11)
Freedom	4.5(1)	4.7(1)	4.9(3)	6.5(4)	6.9(7)	5.6(1)	6.0(3)
Happiness	4.7(2)	6.2(2)	7.5(7)	6.0(3)	4.4(2)	6.2(3)	7.3(9)
Inner harmony	7.4(6)	8.8(9)	7.7(8)	10.9(13)	3.3(1)	7.4(7)	6.5(5)
Mature love	5.6(3)	7.4(6)	6.6(5)	6.5(5)	4.4(3)	7.1(6)	6.6(6)
National security	16.6(17)	13.8(17)	13.9(17)	5.6(2)	16.4(17)	13.5(15)	13.7(14)
Pleasure	12.3(14)	13.1(15)	12.7(14)	11.2(14)	13.6(15)	15.4(18)	14.3(17)
Salvation	17.6(18)	13.4(16)	15.9(18)	15.9(18)	17.6(18)	12.7(12)	13.8(15)
Self-respect	6.9(4)	7.0(4)	7.5(6)	9.7(11)	5.6(5)	6.5(4)	6.9(8)
Social recognition	13.9(16)	12.9(14)	13.7(16)	13.5(16)	13.7(16)	14.7(17)	14.3(18)
True friendship	7.3(5)	8.7(8)	4.9(2)	10.1(12)	5.5(4)	7.0(5)	4.8(1)
Wisdom	8.3(8)	6.8(3)	4.7(1)	7.3(6)	5.9(6)	6.0(2)	5.3(2)

Figures shown are median rankings and, in parentheses, composite rank orders.

TABLE 6

Instrumental value medians and composite rank orders for Canadian, American, and Australian college men and women, and for Israeli college men

	Men				Women		
	Canadian N = 125	American N = 169	Australian N = 279	Israeli N = 71	Canadian N = 133	American N = 129	Australian N = 184
Ambitious	9.4(11)	6.4(3)	7.8(6)	8.7(7)	11.4(12)	8.2(5)	9.9(12)
Broadminded	6.4(4)	6.7(4)	4.6(2)	9.2(9)	6.7(5)	6.7(4)	5.5(3)
Capable	9.9(12)	7.5(5)	8.2(8)	6.5(4)	10.9(11)	10.8(13)	9.8(11)
Cheerful	8.8(6)	12.0(15)	8.5(9)	12.2(14)	7.5(6)	10.3(11)	7.7(7)
Clean	15.4(17)	14.1(17)	13.9(17)	12.6(15)	13.9(17)	14.4(17)	13.4(17)
Courageous	9.1(8)	8.4(8)	8.7(10)	9.8(12)	10.2(10)	8.3(6)	7.4(5)
Forgiving	9.1(10)	10.5(12)	9.3(11)	14.3(18)	6.5(4)	8.7(7)	7.6(6)
Helpful	9.1(9)	11.9(14)	10.2(13)	9.3(10)	9.3(8)	8.9(8)	9.3(10)
Honest	3.0(1)	5.2(1)	4.0(1)	5.1(1)	1.5(1)	3.4(1)	2.4(1)
Imaginative	10.6(15)	10.8(13)	11.5(15)	13.1(16)	12.6(15)	12.2(15)	12.0(15)
Independent	6.9(5)	7.7(6)	7.9(7)	9.9(13)	9.7(9)	9.1(9)	8.5(8)
Intellectual	8.9(7)	8.5(9)	10.6(14)	7.7(6)	9.1(7)	10.7(12)	11.1(13)
Logical	10.5(14)	8.3(7)	9.9(12)	5.9(3)	12.3(14)	12.1(14)	12.9(16)
Loving	6.4(3)	9.1(11)	7.5(4)	9.1(8)	3.9(2)	5.9(2)	5.6(4)
Obedient	16.6(18)	15.0(18)	15.3(18)	13.6(17)	16.0(18)	15.6(18)	15.1(18)
Polite	14.6(16)	13.2(16)	12.1(16)	9.7(11)	13.3(16)	12.7(16)	11.5(14)
Responsible	5.6(2)	5.9(2)	5.2(3)	5.2(2)	5.3(3)	6.1(3)	4.5(2)
Self-controlled	10.2(13)	8.6(10)	7.7(5)	7.6(5)	11.6(13)	9.1(10)	9.3(9)

Figures shown are median rankings and, in parentheses, composite rank orders.

REFERENCES

APA Monitor. 1972. 'Should Psychologists Tell Test Results to Clients? ', 3, p. 17

Anderson, C.C. and A.D.J. Côté. 1966. 'Belief Dissonance as a Source of Disaffection Between Ethnic Groups,' *Journal of Personality and Social Psychology*, 4, pp.447-53

Bakan, D. 1966. 'The Test of Significance in Psychological Research,' *Psychological Bulletin*, 66, pp.423-37

Bandura, A. 1969. *Principles of Behavior Modification.* New York, Holt, Rinehart and Winston

Bishop, G.F., A.M. Barclay and M. Rokeach. 1972. 'Presidential Preferences and Freedom-Equality Value Patterns in the 1968 American Campaign,' *Journal of Social Psychology*, 88, pp.207-12

Burton, A. 1969. *Encounter: The Theory and Practice of Encounter Groups.* San Francisco, Jossey-Bass

Campbell, J.P. and M.D. Dunnette. 1968. 'Effectiveness of T-Group Experiences in Managerial Training and Development,' *Psychological Bulletin*, 70, pp.73-104

Cochrane, R. 1971. 'The Structure of Value Systems in Male and Female Prisoners,' *British Journal of Criminology*, 11, pp.73-9

Ellis, A. 1962. *Reason and Emotion in Psychotherapy.* New York, Lyle Stuart

Feather, N.T. 1970. 'Educational Choice and Student Attitudes in Relation to Terminal and Instrumental Values,' *Australian Journal of Psychology*, 22, pp.127-44

Feather, N.T. and G. Wasyluk. 1973. 'Subjective Assimilation Among Ukrainian Migrants: Value Similarity and Parent-Child Differences,' *Australian and New Zealand Journal of Sociology*, 9

Gardner, R.C. and W.E. Lambert. 1972. *Attitudes and Motivation in Second-Language Learning.* Rowley, Mass., Newbury House

Glasser, W. 1965. *Reality Therapy.* New York, Harper and Row

Gordon, M.M. 1964. *Assimilation in American Life.* New York, Oxford University Press

Hadamard, J. 1945. *The Psychology of Invention in the Mathematical Field.* New York, Dover

Hague, W. 1968. 'Value Systems and Vocational Choice of the Priesthood.' Unpublished PhD dissertation, University of Alberta Library, University of Alberta

Hollen, C.C. 1972. 'Value Change, Perceived Instrumentality, and Attitude Change.' Unpublished PhD dissertation, Michigan State University Library, Michigan State University

Janis, I.L. and L. Mann. 1965. 'Effectiveness of Emotional Role Playing in Modifying Smoking Habits and Attitudes,' *Journal of Experimental Research in Personality*, 1, pp.84-90

Lewin, K. and P. Grabbe. 1945. 'Conduct, Knowledge, and Acceptance of New Values,' *Journal of Social Issues*, 1, pp. 53-64

Lipset, S.M. 1963. 'The Value Patterns of Democracy: A Case Study in Comparative Analysis,' *American Sociological Review*, 28, pp.515-31

Lundy, J.R. 1972. 'Increasing Personal Relevance as a Means of Enhancing Academic Performance: An Empirical Study.' PhD thesis in progress

Mann, L. and I.L. Janis. 1968. 'A Follow-Up Study of the Long-Term Effects of Emotional Role Playing,' *Journal of Personality and Social Psychology*, 8, pp.339-42

Martin, B.M.E. 1964. 'Ethnic Group and Belief as Determinants of Social Distance.' Unpublished Master's thesis, University of Western Ontario, London, Canada

Moreno, J.L. 1946. *Psychodrama*. New York, Beacon

Mowat, F. 1968. *People of the Deer*. New York, Pyramid

Proshanksy, H.M. 'Some Reflections of a New President,' *SPSSI Newsletter*, 132, p.1

Rim, Y. 1970. 'Values and Attitudes,' *Personality*, 1, 243-50

Rogers, C.R. 1959. 'A theory of Therapy, Personality, and Interpersonal Relationships, as Developed in the Client-Centered Framework,' *Psychology: A Study of a Science, Vol. 3*, S. Koch, ed. New York, McGraw-Hill

Rokeach, M. 1965. 'In Pursuit of the Creative Process,' *The Creative Organization*, Gary Steiner, ed. Glencoe, Ill., Free Press

– 1967. *Value Survey*. Sunnyvale, Calif., Halgren Tests

– 1968. *Beliefs, Attitudes, and Values*. San Francisco, Jossey-Bass

– 1969. 'Value Systems in Religion,' *Review of Religious Research*, 11, pp.3-23

– 1971. 'Long-Range Experimental Modification of Values, Attitudes, and Behavior,' *American Psychologist*, 26, pp.453-9

– 1973. *The Nature of Human Values*. New York, Free Press

Rokeach, M., M.G. Miller and J.A. Snyder. 1971. 'The Value Gap Between Police and Policed,' *Journal of Social Issues*, 27, pp.155-71

Rokeach, M. and S. Parker. 1970. 'Values as Social Indicators of Poverty and Race Relations in America,' *The Annals of the American Academy of Political and Social Science*, 388, pp.97-111

Sanford, N. 1970. 'Whatever Happened to Action Research?', *Journal of Social Issues*, 26, pp.3-23

Sanford, N., ed. 1971. *Sanctions for Evil*. San Francisco, Jossey-Bass

Siegel, S. 1956. *Nonparametric Statistics for the Behavioral Sciences*. New York, McGraw-Hill

Silverman, B.I., J. Jaffe and G.F. Bishop. 1972. 'The Values of Psychology Graduate Students,' unpublished manuscript

Skinner, B.F. 1971. *Beyond Freedom and Dignity*. New York, Knopf

Stehr, N. and L.E. Larson. 1972. 'The Rise and Decline of Areas of Specialization,' *American Sociologist*, 7, pp.3 and 5-6

Vidmar, N. and M. Rokeach. 1973. 'Archie Bunker's Bigotry: Perceptions in the

Eye of the Beholder,' Annual Meetings of the Eastern Psychological Association, May 3-5, 1973. Washington, D.C.

White, R.W. 1959. 'Motivation Reconsidered: The Concept of Competence,'
Psychological Bulletin, 66, pp.297-333

Commentary W.P. ARCHIBALD

As a sociologically oriented social psychologist I find Dr Rokeach's
interest in values rather than more specific attitudes refreshing for a
number of reasons. In the first place, in the attitude literature in social
psychology there has been a fetishism for *form* to the determent of
content. By this I mean that the content of the attitudes studied is
usually regarded as irrelevant, and that instead the focus has been upon
the positivity or negativity or moderation or extremity of the attitudes.
As a consequence, researchers have had a propensity to equate such
things as the desire to learn nonsense syllables or brush one's teeth with
racially prejudiced attitudes or any number of other more important
attitudes. This emphasis upon 'theoretical relevance', to use Dr
Rokeach's terms, not only decreases the 'social' and 'technical' relevance of these research traditions from the standpoint of non-social-
scientists, but also gives the researcher himself an excuse for not using
his research in his personal and political life. It also fails to excite many
students because contentless traditions of attitude research have little
'personal relevance' to them. By focusing upon general values Dr
Rokeach does not necessarily completely circumvent that form vs content dilemma, but his work does indeed lead one to consider content. Consequently, for example, through the rankings of 'cleanliness',
'freedom' or 'equality' we can perhaps determine the relative importance to people of brushing their teeth and being prejudiced towards
others.

Secondly, the shift to a concern with content raises a question of
particular importance to sociologists: that is, the question of the social
sources of people's values. Thus, for example, Dr Rokeach is rather
naturally led to compare the values of college professors with those of

the general population, and when he finds that the former group values a sense of accomplisment more and a comfortable life less, he is rather naturally led to conclude that 'this difference ... must be attributed to socio-economic differences ... ' Unfortunately, Dr Rokeach was not compelled to stress that this difference probably does not arise because college professors have 'better' values, but because *having* higher salaries, control over their work, and comfortable lives, they can at least verbally concern themselves with the so-called 'better things in life'. Large numbers of the general population can achieve neither a sense of accomplishment nor a comfortable life, and have to settle instead for being clean and obedient (Kohn and Schooler 1969).

Thirdly and finally, the study of values leads one rather naturally to reflect upon the validity of the most popular general theories in the social sciences; their values play a prominent part because social structure itself is usually defined as a pattern of values. Thus the 'structural functional' model of society, which finds most of its adherence in anthropology and sociology, includes the assumption that most people in a society have similar values and that it is this underlying *value consensus* which holds society together. Similarly, in the 'pluralist' model of society, more popular than the functional model in sociology and still more popular in economics and political science, it is assumed that interest groups compete on the basis of contradictory values, but that there is agreement on the so-called 'rules of the game' which are collectively defined by the word 'democracy'.

I would argue, however, that it is precisely when one tries to explain similarities and differences in general values that one can be most easily misled by available empirical evidence, and that for these reasons research with very general values must be rigorously supplemented with research on values whose level of abstraction is more 'middle range'. Let me briefly suggest some of the dangers and the evidence which I feel justifies this concern.

In the first place, I would argue that if one concentrates upon general values one is likely to overemphasize the amount of value consensus and underestimate the amount of conflict in a society. Let's take an example from Dr Rokeach. American social scientists rank 'equality' significantly higher than the general American population does, but the two rankings are within three ranks of each other, and the rankings of 'freedom' are identical (Table 1). Does this indicate a great deal of value consensus in the United States? Perhaps, but is this particular value consensus an important one? In the first place, such values are 'motherhood and apple pie' ones. But more importantly, they are so abstract and so loosely tied to specific norms and behaviour that very contradictory acts could be interpreted as being consistent with the same general value (see Mann 1970). For example, management views picketing, which prevents non-striking workers from coming to work, as an 'undemocratic' practice because it denies some individuals the basic right to work, but striking workers view 'scabbing' as 'undemocratic' because individual 'scabs', often outsiders, are rejecting the decision of the majority of workers to strike.

Were researchers to ask white- and blue-collar people to rank the importance of middle range values such as those implied in statements like 'Big business has too much power' or 'Trade unions have too much power', they would find rather clear class differences, as sociologists have indeed found in Britain and the United States (for example, Goldthorpe *et al.* 1969; Kornhouser 1965). In a general review of the evidence for and against the claim for value consensus in those two countries, Michael Mann (1970) concludes that there is very little of it, except with regard to general motherhood and apple pie values.

Secondly, however, I would argue that even concentrating upon middle range values, let alone general values, can easily mislead one into thinking that if one knows a person's values one has a good basis for predicting and explaining his behaviour. Dr Rokeach tells us that some of the values in his scale correlate significantly with certain kinds of overt behaviour. However, if these correlations are even as high as those between specific attitudes and behaviour, then they are at best moderate, and when the direction of situational pressures conflicts with the direction of personal attitudes, the former win out. In the studies to which I refer, racially prejudiced individuals admit members of other races to their hotels and restaurants (Kutner *et al.* 1951), and racially unpredjudiced white students will not agree to have their picture taken with black students if these pictures could imply intimacy and are to be published (Warner and DeFleur 1969). Similarly, people take no particular offense at misrepresenting themselves if they gain by it

(Gergen 1968), and convincing others about the value of brushing one's teeth or weaning one's child is not likely to be followed by actual behavioural changes (Festinger 1964).

What one *does* find is that the reverse relationship appears to be more useful; that is, a person's values appear to *derive from* his position in the social structure and the interpersonal pressures he encounters in his usual activities. Leiberman (1956), for instance, finds that workers promoted to foremen become more pro-management and more anti-union, whereas workers promoted to union steward become more anti-management and more pro-union. This relationship seems to hold with some general values as well. Is it surprising, for example, that Dr Rokeach's business professors value equality less social scientists do (p.160)? I don't think so. The greater value placed on being logical by college professors and middle-class people in general (p.159), furthermore, can probably be explained by the fact that there is no need for consistency if one does not have the power to act upon one's values. This contention is supported by a reasonable amount of evidence, ranging from Robert Zajonc's classic study (1960) of the effects of having to communicate as opposed simply to listening to studies indicating that political activists are more consistent in their values than the politically inactive (see Mann 1970).

This implies that people should be judged more on their actions than on their words since 'actions' do in fact 'speak louder'. Since this clearly applies to the verbally sophisticated university community as well as to the population at large, we must ask whether social scientists still remain a source of progressive change. Perhaps so, but if getting involved in politics is considered, the halo over the head of social scientists shrinks considerably. Note, by the way, Professor Rokeach's justifiable disappointment at finding that college professors rank courageous lower than the general U.S. population does.

Thirdly and finally, if values can in fact be best understood as reactions to and rationalizations of one's own interests, then it follows that if one is to understand a person through his values it helps to know his everyday experiences and the desires he has or has not the power to fulfil.

Earlier I intimated that social scientists may have difficulty understanding the basis for value differences between themselves and less fortunate people because of class differences in experiences and power.

In spite of its obvious touchiness, I think one should also raise at this point the issue of the relationship between Canadian and American values. In doing so, let me say that it is a credit to Dr Rokeach's personal objectivity that he notes some important value differences between his sample of Canadian and American undergraduates.

Why is it that the Canadians rank *a sense of accomplishment, ambitious* and *capable,* and *self-controlled* and *logical* lower and *equality, freedom,* and *independence* higher? Dr Rokeach is indeed correct in observing that these results cannot be explained by the claim that Canadians are simply more conservative than Americans, as Lipset and others have been all but ready to proclaim. Nor can they be explained by the fact that Canadians have different house designs or curtains, as one is apparently suppose to gather from listening to Dr Margaret Mead.

Here any number of a host of Canadian social scientists can tell us that Canadians have always acted peculiarly because their experiences have been peculiar when compared to those of Britons or Americans. In part because Canada has had a continuous colonial status and in part because its indigenous economic elite is a 'chip off the old British block', Canada's class structure is somewhat more rigid than that of the United States. As a consequence, Canada has had both more Toryism *and* more socialist sentiment than the United States, *in spite of* the domination of Canadian unions by American Gomperites.[1] Canadians have fewer illusions about making it to the top than Americans do, in part because the opportunities for doing so are less. Undoubtedly this pessimism is an important factor in explaining Canada's underdevelopment, but it is important to remember that it is Canadians' experiences of their social structure which produce this pessimism in the first place, and if it appears as if the structure is to remain intact, there is no particular reason to revise one's estimates.

To date there is no comprehensive study of the effects of the structure of Canada upon these particular Canadian values, but at the same time there is enough evidence to justify pursuing the matter. In her presentation of a well-known interpretation of Canadian literature, for example, Margaret Atwood (1972) documents a peculiarly obsessive concern among Canadian writers with failure and death. Similarly, there is much more evidence for what I take to be the more healthy and hopeful side of the Canadian ambivalency than continentalists on both sides of the border would have us believe. In the results of a 1972 Gallup poll, for example, 40 per cent of the Canadians interviewed said the Canadian government was not doing enough about American domination of Canada's industry and natural resources, 34 per cent said they approved of the government's policy, and 26 per cent weren't sure. Similarly, in their study of 2,000 south-western Ontatio high-school students Harvey, Hunter-Harvey and Vance (1972) found that fully 76.5 per cent stated at least a moderate desire for national independence. *If* Canadian social scientists are as progressive as Dr Rokeach implies they are, perhaps they should catch up with the people they claim to be leading.

NOTE

1 For external sources of Canada's social structure, see particularly the work of Innis and Davis, which is referred to in a 'quick and dirty' discussion by Kathleen Herman (1972). For more stress on internal sources see S.D. Clark, also referred to by Herman. A brief and lucid presentation of this type of argument can be found in Horowitz (1968, pp.3-57).

REFERENCES

Atwood, Margaret. 1972. *Survival: A Thematic Guide to Canadian Literature.* Toronto, Anansi

Festinger, L. 1964. 'Behavioural Support for Opinion Change,' *Public Opinion Quarterly*, 28, pp.404-17

Gergen, K.J. 1968. 'Personal Consistency and the Presentation of Self,' *The Self in Social Interaction, Vol. 1*, C. Gordon and K.J. Gergen, eds. New York, John Wiley & Sons. Pp.299-308

Goldthorpe, John H., David Lockwood, Frank Bechhofer and Jennifer Platt. 1969. *The Affluent Worker in the Class Structure.* Cambridge, Cambridge University Press

Harvey, Ted G., Susan K. Hunter-Harvey and W. George Vance. 1972. 'Nationalist Sentiment among Canadian Adolescents.' Unpublished paper, University of Western Ontario

Herman, Kathleen. 1972. 'Canadian Society,' *Read Canadian: A Book About Canadian Books*, Robert Fulford, D. Godfrey and A. Rotstein, eds. Toronto, James Lewis & Samuel. Pp. 126-43

Horowitz, Gad. 1968. *Canadian Labour in Politics.* Toronto, University of Toronto Press

Kornhauser, Arthur. 1965. *The Mental Health of the Industrial Worker.* New York, John Wiley & Sons

Kutner, Bernard, Carol Wilkins and Penny Yarrow. 1952. 'Verbal Attitudes and Overt Behavior Involving Racial Prejudice,' *Journal of Abnormal Social Psychology*, 47, pp.649-52

Lieberman, S. 1956. 'The Effects of Changes in Roles on the Attitudes of Role Occupants,' *Human Relations*, 9, pp.385-402

Mann, M. 1970. 'The Social Cohesion of Liberal Democracy,' *American Sociological Review*, 35, pp.423-39

Warner, L.G., and M.L. DeFleur. 1969. 'Attitude as an Interactional Concept: Social Constraint and Social Distance as Intervening Variables Between Attitudes and Action,' *American Sociological Review*, 34, pp.153-69

Zajonc, R.B. 1960. 'The Process of Cognitive Tuning in Communication,' *Journal of Abnormal and Social Psychology*, 61, pp.159-67

CANADIAN UNIVERSITY PAPERBOOKS

Of related interest

Lightning Source UK Ltd.
Milton Keynes UK
UKHW020021210722
406167UK00009B/786

9 780802 062482